Hg2 Marrakech

A Hedonist's guide to
Marrakech

Written and photographed by
Paul Sullivan

A Hedonist's guide to Marrakech

Managing director – Tremayne Carew Pole
Marketing director – Sara Townsend
Series editor – Catherine Blake
Design – Katy Platt
Maps – Richard Hale
Typesetting – Dorchester Typesetting
Repro – PDQ Digital Media Solutions
Printers – Printed in Italy by Printer Trento srl
Publisher – Filmer Ltd
Additional photography – Tremayne Carew Pole, Rob Ditcher

Email – info@hg2.com
Website – www.hg2.com

First Published in the United Kingdom in November 2006 by
Filmer Ltd
47 Filmer Road,
London SW6 7JJ

ISBN – 1-905428-06-5 / 978-1-905428-06-9

Hg2 Marrakech

CONTENTS

How to...		6
Updates		6
The concept		7
MARRAKECH		8
MARRAKECH MAP		
The Medina (North)		12
The Medina (South)		16
Gueliz/Hivernage		20
La Palmeraie		24
SLEEP		28
EAT		70
DRINK		100
SNACK		112
PARTY		124
CULTURE		136
SHOP		148
PLAY		172
INFO		186

How to…

A Hedonist's guide to… is broken down into easy to use sections:
Sleep, Eat, Drink, Snack, Party, Culture, Shop, Play and Info. In each of
these sections you will find detailed reviews and photographs. At the
front of the book you will find an introduction to the city and an
overview map, followed by introductions to the four main areas and
more detailed maps. On each of these maps you will see the places
that we have reviewed, laid out by section, highlighted on the map with
a symbol and a number. To find out about a particular place simply turn
to the relevant section, where all entries are listed alphabetically.
Alternatively, browse through a specific section (e.g. Eat) until you find
a restaurant that you like the look of. Next to your choice will be a
small coloured dot – each colour refers to a particular area of the city.
Simply turn to the relevant map to discover the location.

Updates

Hg2 have developed a network of journalists in each city to review the
best hotels, restaurants, bars, clubs, etc., and to keep track of the latest
developments – new places open up all the time, while others simply
fade away or just go out of style. To access our free updates as well as
the content of each guide, simply log onto our website www.hg2.com
and register. We welcome your help. If you have any comments or
recommendations, please feel free to email us at info@hg2.com.

Book your hotel on Hg2.com

We believe that the key to a great city break is choosing the right
hotel. Our unique site now enables you to browse through our selection of hotels, using the interactive maps to give you a good feel for
the area as well as the nearby restaurants, bars, sights, etc., before you

book. Hg2 has formed partnerships with the hotels featured in our guide to bring them to readers at the lowest possible price. Our site now incorporates special offers from selected hotels, as well as a diary of interesting events taking place, 'Inspire Me'.

The concept

A Hedonist's guide to… is designed to appeal to a more urbane and stylish traveller. The kind of traveller who is interested in gourmet food, elegant hotels and seriously chic bars – the traveller who feels the need to explore, shop and pamper themselves away from the crowds.

Our aim is to give you an insider's knowledge of a city, to make you feel like a well-heeled, sophisticated local and to take you to the most fashionable places in town to rub shoulders with the local glitterati.

In today's world work rules our life, and weekends away are few and far between; when we do manage to get away we want to have as much fun and to relax as much as possible with the minimum amount of stress. This guide is all about maximizing time. There is a photograph of each place we feature, so before you go you know exactly what you are getting into; choose a restaurant or bar that suits you and your needs.

We pride ourselves on our independence and our integrity. We eat in all the restaurants, drink in all the bars and go wild in the nightclubs – all totally incognito. We charge no one for the privilege of appearing in the guide, and every place is reviewed and included at our discretion.

We feel cities are best enjoyed by soaking up the atmosphere: wander the streets, indulge in some retail therapy, re-energize yourself with a massage and then get ready to eat like a king and party hard on the local scene.

Marrakech

One of the most talked-about cities in recent years, Marrakech has become the destination for those interested in design, shopping and the naturally exotic. The centrepiece in what is widely regarded as North Africa's adventure playground, it has brought international sophistication to this dusty, dry corner of the world.

Despite almost 50 years of French occupation and a brisk trade in tourism, the city has maintained a sense of mystery and old-world charm not found anywhere else so close to Europe.

The city was initially founded in 1062 by the Almoravids – a Berber tribe that planted the first palm trees and erected the distinctive Medina walls, which still stand proudly today. Over the next thousand years the city came under the rule of various tribes and peoples: the Almohads (1147–1289), the Merenids (1276–1554), the Saadians (1549–1668) and, between 1912 and 1956, the French.

It was during the Swinging 1960s that Marrakech acquired its bohemian appeal, as the likes of Yves Saint Laurent, The Beatles, The Stones and Jean-Paul Getty all chose to hang out here. Over the ensuing decades increasing numbers of style-conscious ex-pats came to the city to invest their money and design ideas, thus creating the mix of ancient tradition and modern chic that epitomizes the place today. Its sophisticated *riads*, influenced and inspired by Islamic art but also by practical necessity, continue to captivate visitors with their luxurious, photogenic interiors and indulgent atmosphere.

Meanwhile, the streets of the Medina remain relatively unchanged, providing a rare insight into the lives of ordinary Marrakechi and catapulting visitors back in time. The dust and heat of the Medina streets contrasts markedly with the relative sophistication and Westernization of Gueliz and other, newer, parts of the city.

There are many ways to spend a perfect day and night in the city. You could wander the ancient Medina streets in the morning, soaking up the bustling, ramshackle, pre-industrial atmosphere, hunting down some bargains and visiting a museum or Medersa. You could take a lunch break in one of the refined eateries that lie behind the Medina's dusty doors. Afterwards, head to Gueliz to check out an art gallery or treat yourself to some new clothes in the city's boutiques.

In the evening, indulge in the full grandeur of the Moroccan dining experience at one of the palace restaurants, then take a refreshing mint tea at a café on the Jemaa el Fna and marvel at the nocturnal madness that has been unfolding in a similar way for the last thousand years. When the night is done, head back to your quiet, comfortable *riad* for a sound night's sleep, full of Arabian dreams.

If you feel the need to get out of the city, then there is a wealth of adventure open to you. The High Atlas Mountains are a mere 40km from Marrakech – an hour's taxi ride will see you firmly ensconced among them. Here you can ride, trek, ski or simply soak up the purity of the air and inhale the natural aromas. In spring, wild flowers cover the mountainsides while in autumn the smells of the fruit harvest assail the senses.

A little further away you can begin to explore the edges of the Sahara. The desert is spectacular: its shape-shifting sand dunes and stunning rock formations will take your breath away. You can also make the most of this unique opportunity to observe the semi-nomadic lifestyles of the people who live here.

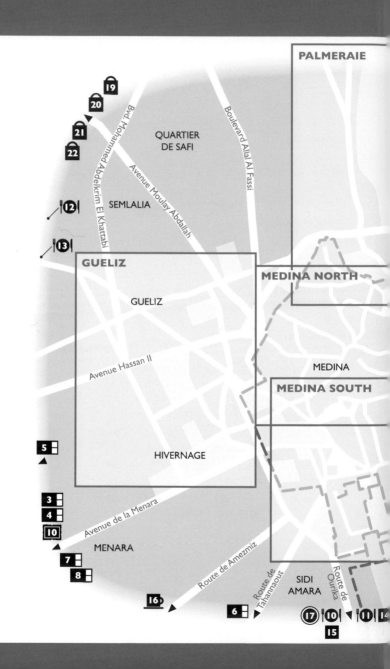

Marrakech city map

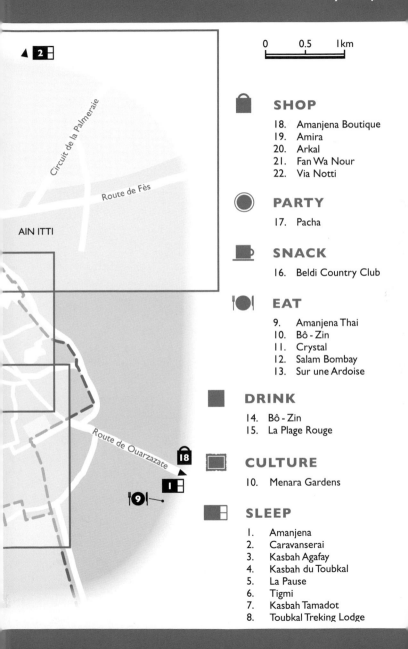

0   0.5   1km

SHOP

18. Amanjena Boutique
19. Amira
20. Arkal
21. Fan Wa Nour
22. Via Notti

PARTY

17. Pacha

SNACK

16. Beldi Country Club

EAT

9. Amanjena Thai
10. Bô - Zin
11. Crystal
12. Salam Bombay
13. Sur une Ardoise

DRINK

14. Bô - Zin
15. La Plage Rouge

CULTURE

10. Menara Gardens

SLEEP

1. Amanjena
2. Caravanserai
3. Kasbah Agafay
4. Kasbah du Toubkal
5. La Pause
6. Tigmi
7. Kasbah Tamadot
8. Toubkal Treking Lodge

Circuit de la Palmeraie

Route de Fès

AIN ITTI

Route de Ouarzazate

The Medina (North)

It's here, within the dense, claustrophobic atmosphere of the Old City, enclosed by its ancient walls, that the majority of visitors to Marrakech spend their time. Here, the magic and mystery of traditional Moroccan life reveal themselves in everyday hustle and bustle.

The endless parade of street traders, cart-pulling donkeys, sweating artisans, blind beggars, playful children and assorted mysterious figures seems frozen in time – and in some ways it is. You may find that initially the exotic sights and distinctive smells of the Medina overwhelm you, but a couple of hours are usually all you need to adapt.

The biggest draws in the northern section of the Old City are the Jemaa el Fna and the souks, as well as historic sights such as the Koutoubia Mosque and the stunning Ben Youssef Medersa.

Of course, one of the most memorable adventures can be yours by simply surrendering yourself to the vicissitudes of the maze. Strolling down nameless street after nameless street (the locals will soon let you know if you've wandered somewhere you shouldn't), you can dis-

cover unique ways of life that will leave a permanent impression on your imagination.

It's here in the Medina that the *riad* boom began – intimate conversions of traditional homes with picturesque courtyards, run as *maisons d'hôte*. *Riads* offer a particular kind of tranquillity and refuge from the bustling alleyways and souks that is not found elsewhere in the city. There are several wonderful examples of these, notably Riad Farnatchi, Riad el Fenn and Riad Tchaikana.

The Medina's policy regarding alcohol is not as relaxed as elsewhere in Marrakech, since it is the Old City and home to some of the most important mosques. Here alcohol can only be found in the hotel bars (in the Jardins de la  Koutoubia and the Mamounia, for example), or in restaurants. Speaking of restaurants, there are some fabulous places to visit, many of them set in beautiful old buildings, with gurgling fountains and tables covered in rose petals – opulence and romance are the bywords here. While you are in Marrakech, visits to Le Tobsil, Dar Moha or Dar Marjana are highly recommended.

For many, the Medina's greatest attraction are the souks. Row upon row of tiny stalls, clustered together along narrow twisting alleys, begin to fan out from the northern section of the Jemaa el Fna and never seem to stop. Shopping in the souks is one of the most quintessential Marrakech activities, although those without much experience would do well to practise their haggling skills beforehand.

CULTURE

29. Ben Youssef Medersa
30. Musée de Marrakech

SNACK

26. Café Arabe
27. Café des Epices
28. Dar Cherifa /
    Café Literaire

Diour Jdad

18

21

Rue Bab Taghzout

Rue el Gza

D. Lamsaubre

D. S. Bou Amar

15

Rue Riad Laârous

A. Riad Laârous

3

12

Ave. Fatima Zohra

19

2

5

Rue Dar el Bacha

49

23

14

20

46

36

4

6

Rue Dar el Bacha

47

41

26

28

13

45

Rue Sidi el Yamani

43

44

34

33

Avenue Fatima

1

8

25

38

R. Jbel Lakhdar

Zohra

24

Jemaa el Fna

EAT

19. Dar Marjana
20. Dar Moha
21. Dar Zellij
22. Le Foundouk
23. La Maison Arabe
24. Le Tobsil

The Medina (North) local map

 SLEEP

1. Dar Attajmil
2. Dar Doukkala
3. Dar Saria
4. La Maison Arabe
5. Riad 12
6. Riad 72
7. Riad Azzar
8. Riad el Fenn
9. Riad el Mezouar
10. Riad Enija
11. Riad Farnatchi
12. Riad Kniza
13. Riad Lotus Ambre
14. Riad Lotus Perle
15. Riad Lotus Privelege
16. Tchaikana
17. Riyad el Cadi
18. Ryad Dyor

DRINK

25. Kssour Agafay

SHOP

- Souks
31. Ahmed Ait Taleb
32. Akbar Delights
33. Art Akhnif
34. Art & Deco
35. Artisan el Koutoubia
36. Atelier Moro
37. Bazaar les Palmiers
38. Beldi
39. Bellawi
40. Creation et Passementerie
41. Galerie Mourjana
42. Hassan Makchad
43. Kainkila Bougage
44. Kif Kif
45. Kulchi
46. Les Lamps D'Aladin
47. La Maison du Kaftan Morocain
48. Milouad el Jouli
49. Mustapha Blaoui

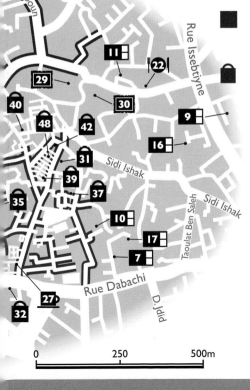

The Medina (South)

The southern half of the Medina is slightly calmer than the north. While there are still twisting *derb*s and winding alleyways, the workshops and souks are less apparent while the residential areas are more so; seemingly, this area is the more affluent.

Like the north, however, it is filled with interesting sights and sounds. The Bahia Palace, the Saadian Tombs, the Royal Palace and the Agdal Gardens draw those interested in the history and architecture of the city. Then there's the Koutoubia, visible from virtually all parts the city, and the convenient meeting-place and non-stop circus that is the Jemaa el Fna.

Some of Marrakech's finest *riads* and hotels are found here in the south, including the legendary Mamounia hotel, the luxurious Villa des Orangers, the elegant Dar les Cigognes and the eclectic Riad Dyor. They epitomize the style and design with which the city has become synonymous, and are dedicated to contemplation and relaxation.

The contrast between life inside and outside the Medina is palpable. Within the walls of the Old City, time stands still. Donkeys are still as common as motorbikes, butchers and vendors sell their wares on the dusty streets, and artisans busy themselves with traditional crafts.

Indulging in a *hammam/gommage* is a must for all visitors to Marrakech. A weekly cleansing ritual for locals, many of whom live without showers and baths in their homes, is essential for personal hygiene. The local *hammams* can be daunting for strangers at first, but people are incredibly welcoming and there is always someone to guide you through the process if you are unsure what to do.

If you prefer luxury and pampering over local experience, head for the Bains de Marrakech – an upmarket spa annexed to the wonderful Riad Mehdi. This is a great place to rejuvenate and de-stress.

There are plenty of restaurants in this lower half of the Medina, such as the wonderfully traditional Dar Zellij, and of course the funky Koz'i Bar, which serves up fabulous sushi. Alternatively, perhaps you would like to learn how to cook some tasty Moroccan food for yourself? If so, Souk Cuisine offers simple but memorable cooking classes in the heart of the southern Medina.

SNACK

22. Café de France
23. Nid' Cigogne
24. Patisserie de Princes

PARTY

25. La Mamounia Casino

SLEEP

1. Dar les Cigognes
2. Les Jardins de la Koutoubia
3. Maison Mnabha
4. La Mamounia
5. Riad Ifoulki
6. Riad Kaiss
7. Riad Mabrouka
8. Riad Mehdi
9. Riad W
10. La Sultana
11. Villa des Orangers

PLAY

38. Bains de Marrakech

The Medina (South) local map

DRINK
19. Churchill's Piano Bar
20. Kozybar
21. The Piano Bar

EAT
12. Narwama
13. Les Jardins de la Koutoubia
14. Les Jardins de la Medina
15. Jemaa el Fna
16. Kozybar
17. Le Marrakchi
18. La Sultana

SHOP
34. Bijouterie el Yasmine Abdelghani
35. Centre Artisanal
36. Original Design
37. Jamade

CULTURE
26. Badii Palace
27. Bahia Palace
28. Jemaa el Fna
29. Koutoubia Mosque
30. Saadian Tombs
31. Dar Tiskiwin
32. Agdal Gardens
33. Mamounia Gardens

Rue Issebôyne
Sidi Ishak
 shak
Rue Fral Semar
Rue de Bab Aylen
D. Boutouil
Rue Sidi Boulabada
Derb Tbib
D.Jdid
Rue Tihizrit
Rue Douar Graoua
Rue Bab Ahmad
D. Ferran
Avenue Qadi Ayad
5
D.Jdid
ue Douar Graoua
Jnane Ben Chegra
7
31
27
Rue Imam el Ghezali
1
32

0   250   500m

Gueliz/Hivernage

Gueliz – the New City – was constructed in 1913, soon after the French took power. The broad, European-style avenues and boulevards convey a sense of space, order and cleanliness a world away from the intricate, odorous chaos of the Medina.

This very Westernized quarter – which borders Hivernage, ostensibly an extension of Gueliz – is home to the business community. Alongside the financial institutions, post offices and other economic franchises, however, is an attractive array of restaurants, bars, galleries and clubs.

Much of the city's nightlife is located in this area, since the licensing restrictions are much more relaxed here than they are in the Medina. Local drinking spots include chill-out bar Le Lounge, Le Comptoir, Montecristo and the opulent Jad Mahal. It's also a short taxi ride from these bars to nightclubs such as VIP, Diamant Doir, Paradise and Theatro, where you can party on until 4am.

Gueliz/Hivernage is also home to some of the city's best restaurants, cafés and art galleries. The restaurant scene is particularly vibrant:

dinner at the opulent Jad Mahal is an exercise in style and people-watching, while Lolo Quoi, Kech Mara or El Fassia offer fantastic food in unique surroundings.

There are plenty of shopping options too – for hipsters and tradition-alists alike – and strolling casually along Mohammed V and its various arteries can provide pleasant respite from the intensity of the souks. Galleries in the area show new Moroccan art, clothes designers put contemporary twists on traditional styles, and furniture and antique stores allow you to realize your vision of your very own *riad* interior once you get home.

Although there's not much here for the sightseer, it's perfectly possible to spend a memorable day or evening (or both) in Gueliz, taking a sophisticated breakfast at the Grand Café de la Poste or the Café du Livre (or more traditional fare at Les Negoçiants), visiting the Majorelle Gardens, or the central market (Marché Central) and then heading to one of the many restaurants, bars or clubs come night-time.

A *petit taxi* between the Medina and Gueliz costs around 10dh and takes around 5 minutes.

Bvd. Mohammed Abdelkrim el Khattabi

Bvd Zahal Ben Ahmed

Rue Abdelouahab Derra

Rue Erraouda

Avenue de la 47e DMM

Avenue de France

Rue du Lieutenant Lamure

Rue Capitaine Arrigui

Rue du Draâ

R. Ibn Zaydoun

Rue Allal Ben Ahmed

Rue Ibn Aicha

Bvd. Mohammed Zerktouni

Rue Tarik Iben Ziyad

Rue Sourya

Rue Ibn Toumment

Ave. Yacoub

Bvd. El Mansour Eddahbi

Boulevard Mohammed V

Rue el Imam

Rue Mohammed el Beqal

Bvd. Moulay Rachid

Rue de Mauritanie

Avenue Hassan II

Rue de Yougoslavie

Boulevard Al Hancali

Rue Moulay Hassan 1er

Avenue el Qadissia

SHOP

30. El Badil
31. La Porte d'Orient
32. L'Orientalist
33. Gallerie Bleu
34. Marrakech Arts Gallery
35. Matisse Gallery
36. Centre Commercial
37. Ensemble Artisanal
38. Atika
39. Casa Mangani
40. Scenes du Lin
41. Ambience & Styles
42. Interieur 29
43. Lun'Art Gallery
44. Maison de Bali
45. Azziza
46. Gallerie Birkemeyer
47. Michele Bacconier
48. Yahya

SNACK

14. Amandine
15. Boule de Neige
16. Café du Livre
17. Café Les Negociants
18. Grand Café de la Poste

0   250   500m

DRINK

10. Le Comptoir
11. Jad Mahal
12. Le Lounge
13. Montecristo

EAT

1. Bagatelle
2. Le Comptoir
3. El Fassia
4. Le Jacaranda
5. Jad Mahal
6. Hadika
7. Kech Mara
8. Le Square
9. La Trattoria di Giancarlo

PLAY

49. Les Secrets de Marrakech Spa

PARTY

19. Diamant Noir
20. Jad Mahal
21. Montecristo
22. Paradise
23. Theatro
24. Totem
25. VIP
26. Es Saadi Casino

CULTURE

27. Gallerie d'Art Lawrence-Arnott
28. Musée d'Art Islamique
29. Majorelle Gardens

La Palmeraie

A 15-minute drive outside the old city, La Palmeraie is famous for its eponymous palm trees and for the wealth of luxury accommodation (public and private) that exists here.

A dusty and arid suburb of Marrakech, it has evolved organically and somewhat haphazardly. It is home to spacious hotel complexes, including some wonderfully opulent oases of decadence, and some of the finest golf courses that Morocco has to offer.

The standard of accommodation available here makes La Palmeraie an attractive option for those wishing to be close to Gueliz and the Medina yet at the same time a million miles away.

The ramshackle, old-world charm of places such as Ayniwen offer exclusivity and privacy, while catering for your every whim. Alternatively, there's the unparalleled luxury of Jnane Tamsna and Dar Zemora, both of which offer stunning gardens, azure pools and an air of exotic refinement.

The Palmeraie Golf Palace is also located here. Not only does it have an excellent golf course and a good riding stable, but it also boasts the über-chic Nikki Beach.

Other challenging golf courses can be found at Amelkis and the Royal Golf Club, which host national and international tournaments. Another

recent addition to the ever-growing list of Palmeraie addresses is the stunning Beldi Country Club, an enchanting spot that has a café, restaurant, pool and artisan workshop all in one place.

Unless you're staying here, fancy a round of golf, or want to spend an afternoon at Nikki Beach or the Beldi, there's little reason to visit La Palmeraie. If you can manage just one of these, however, you won't leave disappointed.

0   0.5   1km

EAT

6. L'Abyssin
7. Jnane Tamsna
8. Ksar Char - Bagh

PARTY

11. New Feeling

SNACK

10. Nikki Beach

SLEEP

1. Ayniwen
2. Dar Zemora
3. Jnane Tamsna
4. Ksar Char - Bagh
5. Palais Rhoul

DRINK

9. Nikki Beach

SHOP

12. Boutique Indigo
13. Maryanne Loum-Martin
     Boutique

Route de Fès

sleep...

No other city on earth offers as many intoxicating accommodation options as Marrakech. From the tiny and intimate to the vast and ridiculously opulent, the city's sleeperies span snug *maisons d'hôte*, snazzy designer *riads*, pseudo-corporate hotels, sumptuous villas and super-reclusive mansions. In other words, whatever your accommodation requirements, you'll find them met here.

If you're looking to stay in the Medina, you need to know about *riads*: traditional Moroccan houses arranged around an attractive central courtyard and/or garden. In the last few decades an ever-increasing number of ex-pats – mostly European, many of them artists and designers – have bought their own (as well as *dars*, which have a slightly different structure, are often larger and don't necessarily have a courtyard), and transformed them into visions of chic elegance. The Medina's dusty doors conceal a whole range of decorative themes: traditional Moroccan interiors at Riad Ifoulki and Riad Kniza; subtle mixes of the traditional and the trendy at Dar Saria, Riad Farnatchi, Riad Tchaikana, Riad W and Riad Azzar; and grand designer statements at current hotspots such as Riad Perle Lotus, Riad El Fenn or the fabled Riad Enija.

Because *riads* are usually of a relatively small size – most have between four and eight rooms – they offer an intimate *maison d'hôte* experience: burbling fountains, soothing salons, isolated roof terraces and great home cooking (although many are thoroughly equipped with a range of unobtrusive mod-cons, too). These places are thus the perfect choice for those seeking romance and solitude within the hubbub of the ancient city.

Those who wish for a more reclusive experience should look to the Palmeraie. A scruffy, palm-filled area that is home to secluded private residences, luxury villas and grand mansions, it's Marrakech's somewhat sandy and surreal answer to Beverly Hills. It's here, 15 minutes away from the Medina by car, that you'll find the kind of high-end accommodation that attracts the famous and the wealthy. Ayniwen, Dar Zemora, Palais Rhoul and Jnane Tamsna are among the more established places to stay in the Palmeraie, and are all fine examples of the standards one can expect from the accommodation here. Hidden away behind high walls and gated entrances, they all offer expansive gardens, azure swimming pools, architectural flourishes and, more often than not, a full-blown design aesthetic aimed at reawakening dulled senses.

Similar options exist along various routes in and out of the city, some of them up to 45 minutes away. Some of the very finest accommodation lies on these rural fringes: rustic retreats such as Caravanserai and Tigmi, both set in local villages; the charming Kasbah du Toubkal at the foot of the Atlas Mountains; the impressive Ksar Char Bagh; and the notoriously swish Kasbah Agafay. All of these are completely different from each other, yet unparalleled in their own unique way. Staying in any of these places will guarantee you stunning surround- ings, impeccable service

and a first-class holiday that will leave you fully rejuvenated. Please note that although the remoter places have been given a fairly low score in the 'Location' category, this is because of their distance (more than 15 minutes by car/taxi) from the centre of the city. It is of course no reflection on their setting – on the contrary, most offer unbeatable landscapes and surroundings.

It's worth noting that, wherever you stay, you should book ahead in peak seasons – especially if you are opting for the smaller places, which get full quickly and are often let in their entirety to families or groups. Also, rates change according to season. Since places have their own interpretations of these seasonal periods (and some recognize seasons that others don't, such as a 'middle season'), we have listed the lowest 'low-season' price for a standard double room up to the highest 'high-season' price for a suite.

Our top 10 places to stay in Marrakech are:

1. Riad El Fenn
2. Ksar Char-Bagh
3. Palais Rhoul
4. Kasbah Agafay
5. Amanjena
6. Jnane Tamsna
7. Riad Farnatchi
8. Riad Perle Lotus
9. Riad Enija
10. Riad El Cadi

Our top 5 for style are:

1. Riad Perle Lotus
2. Riad El Fenn
3. Riad Farnatchi
4. Riad Enija
5. Jnane Tamsna

Our top 5 for atmosphere are:

1. Ksar Char-Bagh
2. Jnane Tamsna
3. Kasbah Agafay
4. Palais Rhoul
5. Ayniwen

Our top 5 for location are:

1. Villa Des Orangers
2. Riad El Fenn
3. Riad Enija
4. Riad Azzar
5. Les Jardins De La Koutoubia

Amanjena, Route de Ouarzazate, Km 12

Tel: 0 24 40 33 53 www.amanresorts.com
Rates: 8,500–30,000dh

They don't come much more exclusive than this. Part of the Aman Group – one of the foremost luxury hotel chains in the world – the Amanjena is a have-to-see-it-to-believe-it kind of place, a Moroccan palace complex with

Asian overtones set on the outskirts of Marrakech. The dusty pink walls enclose a wonderland of architectural splendour, including a postcard-perfect *basin* (ancient irrigation pool), 39 pavilions, six two-storey *maisons* and one fabulous suite. The rooms are a marvel to behold: imaginatively styled at great expense with flair and panache. Needless to say every kind of exclusive facility and service you could ever need (or imagine) is on offer, from private pools and gardens to personal butlers, plus boutiques, spa, library, two restaurants, tennis courts and a fitness centre. Golfers might also enjoy the fact that the resort is next door to two of the city's three main courses. As is perhaps to be expected, there is an overriding sense of formality at times, but it's a small price to pay for the overall package.

Style 9, Atmosphere 8, Location 7

Ayniwen, Tafrata, Circuit de la Palmeraie, Palmeraie

Tel: 0 24 32 96 84/85 www.dar-ayniwen.com
Rates: 2,000–5,000dh

31

Ayniwen is the kind of place that makes it into Condé Nast Traveller Hot List and attracts reclusive celebrities like Monica Bellucci and Juliette Binoche. Built on two hectares of parkland in the Palmeraie, the main house has a Romanesque grandeur redolent of an 18th-century palace, even though it was constructed as a family house as recently as the late 1970s and only opened to the public six years ago. The four suites in the house look out onto lush gardens, which enclose a heated pool and three addi-

tional private villas (also suites). Décor is deliberately old-fashioned, with an emphasis on local materials and lots of impressive imported antiques, which overwhelm all the mod-cons. Rooms and bathrooms are often huge and have a welcoming, lived-in feel. Intimacy and privacy are ensured at all times and there's a *hammam* and sauna. International and Moroccan cuisine are available on request.

Style 8, Atmosphere 9, Location 7

Caravanserai, 264 Ouled Ben Rahmoune
Tel: 0 24 30 03 02 www.caravanserai.com
Rates: 1,300–4,200dh

If it wasn't for the uniformed man loitering casually at the door and the occasional expensive car parked outside, you could easily mistake Caravanserei for any other traditional village house – from the outside. The 200-year-old building has been renovated in spectacularly authentic fashion, constructed to fit in seamlessly with its surroundings, which happen to be a tiny Arabic village several miles outside Marrakech. As nondescript as the

outside may be, the inside is bursting with the ever-fertile imagination of legendary designer/architect Charles Boccara. The 12 suites and five standard rooms (four doubles, one single) – simple, charming, stylish – are arranged around a courtyard dominated by a large heated pool. Flanking the pool is a cosy restaurant/bar area (Moroccan and French menu) on one side and a small and peaceful designer garden on the other. There's also a *hammam* and assorted terraces offering majestic views of the Atlas and the Palmeraie.

Style 9, Atmosphere 9, Location 7

Dar Attajmil, 23 rue Laksour, Bab Laksour, Medina
Tel: 0 24 42 69 66 www.darattajmil.com
Rates: 800–1,200dh

Settled snugly into the meandering rue Laksour, just next to a small artisan's workshop, Dar Attajmil is run by laid-back Italian fashionista Lucrezia Mutti. Small and intimate, it offers four rooms in the main *riad* plus a newly added double room in a private courtyard next door. Attajmil makes up for its lack of open space with a sense of comfortable homeliness and stylish design. A subtle smell of incense hangs over the frondescent central courtyard, and the nooks and crannies of the maze-like interior have been lovingly and tastefully decorated. The standard rooms are on the poky side but are superbly kitted out with various takes on the Moroccan style and subtle mixes of antique and contemporary furnishings, and the suites are much larger. In addition, the roof terrace is wonderful, boasting a great sunbathing deck and a cute *hammam*/spa (open to the public, reservations essential: see

page 179), where massages, skin treatments and face-masks are all available. Lucrezia can organize everything from treks and *tadelakt* classes to yoga and cooking schools.

Style 8, Atmosphere 8, Location 8

Dar Doukkala, 83 rue Bab Doukkala, Dar el Bacha, Medina
Tel: 0 24 38 34 44 www.dardoukkala.com
Rates: 1,300–3,300dh

Dar Doukkala, named after the ancient neighbourhood in which it's located, opened to the public in January 2003. It's a huge place with six rooms (four rooms, two suites) that unfurl organically around two floors connected by a huge, florid courtyard and a red-and-white tiled stairwell that's like something out of *Alice in Wonderland*; it's just one of the signature flourishes of

designer Jean-Luc Lemée, who has transformed the place into a feast of art-deco curves and madcap orientalism. Things to 'ooh' and 'aah' at include freestanding baths the length of small submarines, cool Plexiglas furnishings and stunningly curvaceous fireplaces. The rooms (which include two suites) are huge, the suites immense, and all are interestingly decorated with his sometimes dizzying combinations of Moroccan and Art Deco styles. The place also has a small *hammam* and a pool. Although it may now be looking a little faded in places, the Dar Doukkala remains one of the more charming options in the Medina.

Style 7, Atmosphere 7, Location 8

Dar les Cigognes, 108 rue de Berima, Medina
Tel: 0 24 38 27 40   www.lescigognes.com
Rates: 1,300–2,500dh

Situated a *baboush*-throw away from the Badii Palace, Les Cigognes is a former 17th-century merchant's townhouse that has been renovated (with the help of star architect Charles Boccara) into a stylish boutique guesthouse. An elegant courtyard (featuring the obligatory citrus trees and gurgling fountain) is the centrepiece, symbolizing a peaceful ambience that's immediately apparent on entering. Around the central courtyard there are subtle public spaces (dining room, library, salon), but the real hipness hangs out in the rooms. There are 11 of them – seven suites, a '*grande chambre*' and a '*chambre luxe*' – all with their own take on Moorish architectural and decorative traditions, and all with en-suite bathrooms with bath and shower facilities. Six of the suites have  been recently added in an adjoining house, together with two more sitting areas, a handicrafts boutique, a *hammam*, a small kitchen and a planted courtyard. A wonderful roof terrace is overlooked by the eponymous storks, and staff are friendly and helpful.

Dar Saria, Derb Ouiahah, 46 Quartier Sidi Abdel Aziz, Medina

Tel: 0 24 42 96 24 www.darsaria.com
Rates: 500–1,000dh

Run by graphic designer Florence and her photographer boyfriend Vincent (both Belgian), Dar Saria is by far the best option for this price range. It was opened in late 2005, freshly converted from the house of a *caid*, and its sensitive restoration has successfully created an aura of low-key elegance. There's no central garden, just a traditional courtyard with a pretty fountain, impressive pillars ('*saria*' means 'pillar'), whitewashed booths, a cute breakfast area, and a beautiful, sprawling bougainvillea plant that scatters red petals all over the floor like something out of a Gabriel Garcia Marquez novel. The four bedrooms are more contemporary, decorated in chocolates

and creams, with Vincent's own arty canvases on the wall. The upstairs suites are big and come with fireplaces and salons, while the downstairs rooms are a little pokier. Close to Dar El Bacha (a section of which is soon to be opened as a museum), the Ben Youssef Medersa and the Musée de Marrakech, this is a great option for young, budget-conscious travellers looking for a romantic, low-key base.

Style 8, Atmosphere 8, Location 8

Dar Zemora, rue El Aandalib, Palmeraie

Tel: 0 24 32 82 00   www.darzemora.com
Rates: 1,500–4,500dh

Owned by a British couple and designed partly by Belgian manageress
Valerie Golinvaux, Dar Zemora is an impressive villa hotel located in the
Palmeraie. Past the main entrance there is a domed reception area that
leads through to a series of eloquent rooms; some have a seasonal theme,
such as the breezy summer Casblanca room and the winter lounge with its

huge fireplace, and there is also a gorgeous dining room with terrace, library
(leather-chairs, WiFi) and a well-cushioned chill-out area known as the Fan
Room, separated from the spacious gardens and fantastic pool by a few
strips of gently wafting coloured fabric. The rest of Zemora is equally entic-
ing. The three en-suite bedrooms are all fantastically decorated in a range of
subtle but seductive Moorish themes, plus there's a honeymoon suite on the
roof (Perla, which comes with its own expansive terrace area) and a separate Zahara suite, which has a four-poster bed, hall, sitting room and its own
private garden. All rooms have marble bathrooms, CD players, and access to
the pool and lawns. There's a spa offering massages and a brand new *hammam*.

Style 8, Atmosphere 8, Location 7

Les Jardins de la Koutoubia, 26 rue de la Koutoubia, Medina

Tel: 0 24 38 88 00 www.lesjardinsdelakoutoubia.com
Rates: 2,400–10,000dh

Les Jardins de la Koutoubia stands on the site of the 13th-century Riad Ouarzazi. The owner – a wealthy French textile manufacturer – was merciless in tearing down what was one of the biggest *riads* in town (it held 25 families), and erecting this giant hotel in its place. By five-star hotel

standards, it boasts the requisite degree of style and intimacy. The wooden, linear reception leads out into a massive courtyard dominated by a huge pool and verdant gardens. The salons around the pool are a talking point, with their traditional furnishings – immense lamps, jewellery, bookcases – created in Brobdingnagian proportions. The rooms, while pleasant enough and boasting all the expected comforts, lack the same sense of innovation and charm, although they are sleek and elegant (in particular the newer suites, which are much bigger). In addition there are two fine restaurants where you can enjoy an inexpensive lunch (see EAT), a wonderful piano bar (see DRINK), a jacuzzi on the roof with views over the Koutoubia, and a spa, *hammam* and fitness centre.

Style 7, Atmosphere 7, Location 9

Jnane Tamsna, Douar Abiad, Palmeraie

Tel: 0 24 32 94 23 www.jnanetamsna.com
Rates: 2,500–4,500dh

Jnane Tamsna is owned by high-profile Marrakech residents Meryanne Loum-Martin (a Senegalese designer) and her husband Gary J. Martin, an American ethno-botanist. One of the more established and well-run properties in the Palmeraie, it has attracted a host of A-list celebrities over the years, including Brad Pitt, David Bowie and Giorgio Armani. The perfect

Moorish arches, grand drawing room and expansive organic gardens are utterly enchanting, conjuring up an idyll of contemporary Moroccan living. The rooms and villas enhance this experience with an inspired mix of ethnic decoration – textiles from Senegal, Berber rugs and Asian silks. A brand new villa – more modern-looking than the others – brings the total amount of rooms to 24, but the pervading sense of exclusion and privacy remains unsullied. As well as a tennis court, several pools and a surprisingly down-to-earth atmosphere, Tamsna also offers wonderful meals that use ingredients taken directly from the gardens (see EAT).

Style 9, Atmosphere 9, Location 7

Kasbah Agafay, Route de Guemassa, 20km
Tel: 0 24 36 86 00 www.kasbahagafay.com
Rates: 4,000–5,000dh

Kasbah Agafay is the brainchild of Moroccan entrepreneur Abel Damoussi. It took three years to buy the Kasbah from its previous 36 owners, and as many years again to restore the building to its current glory. It's one of the most stunning properties in Morocco, sitting on a rise commanding spectacular views across the desert, fields and out to the High Atlas and Jebel

Toubkal, their highest point. Rooms and suites – 20 in total – are built around five main courtyards, connected by a veritable labyrinth of corridors. The décor combines traditional Moroccan with contemporary styles, but it's

the lavish attention to detail that makes Agafay stand out – such as Berber tent poles in the four-poster beds and antique keys as lavatory-paper holders. As well as the bedrooms inside the Kasbah itself there are four tented suites outside whose sides all open out onto the landscape – incredibly romantic if not particularly intimate. A full set of amenities is on offer, including a *hamman*, spa centre (with yoga room), floodlit tennis court, large pool, a divine drawing room and a fabulous restaurant. If you don't want to stay here you can always come for lunch (a 350dh set menu), sign up for a cooking class (see PLAY), use the spa (see PLAY) or all three.

Style 8, Atmosphere 10, Location 7

Kasbah Tamadot, Route d'Imlil, Asni, High Atlas
Tel: 0 44 36 82 00   www.virgin.com/kasbah
Rates: 3,250–11,000dh

Richard Branson's Moroccan retreat, bought in 1999 from antiques dealer Luciano Tempo, opened its doors to the public in February 2005. The position of the hotel, nestling in the meeting-point of two valleys, is stunning; the views of the imperious High Atlas, culminating in the peak of Jbel Toubkal, are quite staggering. The 18 rooms and suites come in a mixture of styles, the product of the energies of various designers ranging from the Branson family and the manager of Vanessa Branson's Riad El Fenn, to Project

Orange, an Old Street architectural and design practice. The Kasbah is more of a destination in itself than it is a base for enjoying Marrakech. Situated an hour and a quarter's drive from the Medina, over sometimes remarkably windy mountain roads,

it is quite cut off from the hubbub of everyday life. Horse-riding in the foothills or even an expedition to the top of Toubkal can be organized if you so desire – but the pace of life here is generally a lot slower than elsewhere. Most people tend to enjoy themselves lounging poolside before rousing themselves to sample the endeavours of the remarkably skilled South African chef, and enjoying the relaxing atmosphere of the spa.

Style 8/9, Atmosphere 8/9, Location 6

Kasbah du Toubkal, Imlil, Asni, High Atlas
Tel: 0 24 48 56 11   www.kasbahdutoubkal.com
Rates: 1,650–8,360dh

The village of Imlil is the starting-point for the ascension of Mount Toubkal, the highest peak in North Africa. There are plenty of backpackers and hotels

in the village, but the Kasbah is without doubt the premier accommodation spot, not just in Imlil, but in the whole of the High Atlas region too. It's a peaceful, rustic mountain retreat with respectable eco-friendly policies (collecting rubbish from local villages, recycling, filtering spring water), and part of the money they receive goes towards local community services such as public *hammams* and village ambulances. There is a range of different sleeping arrangements, from dorms and standard rooms to suites and self-catering-style apartments (with kitchen/living room/all mod-cons). Other amenities include a wonderful restaurant (bring your own alcohol if you want to drink), a *hammam* and plunge pool, and a panoramic roof terrace that looks out over tranquil villages and verdant valleys. Climbs and treks can be arranged through the Kasbah staff; prices range from 25dh for a half-day trek to 200dh (per person) for a full ascent, all with guides, cooks, mules, accommodation and drinks (if required). It's a beautiful way to spend a few days away from the hustle and bustle of the city, and a great place to start and end a Toubkal climb or other High Atlas walk.

Style 8, Atmosphere 9, Location 7

Ksar Char-Bagh, Palmeraie de Marrakech, Palmeraie
Tel: 0 24 32 92 44 www.ksarcharbagh.com
Rates: 5,500–8,500dh

Marrakech has finally found a hotel to rival the Amanjena in terms of pure luxury and indulgence – but with a little more intimacy. Originally owners Patrick and Nicole Levillair were looking for somewhere in the south of France but, unable to find the perfect place, they came to Marrakech to

unwind. They immediately fell in love it, but rather than buying a property they decided to build somewhere spectacular from scratch. Ksar Char-Bagh is styled as a 14th-century Moorish palace, and boasts 12 *harims* (rooms), a *hammam*, swimming pool, first-class restaurant and roof terraces with showers and Berber tents. It was an immediate success – the Levillairs have bewitched the exclusive clientele that Ksar Char-Bagh was designed to attract. The rooms are equipped with silk *djellabas*, bathrobes and toiletries individually fashioned for men and women, and you'll find intricate ornamentation on everything from pillows to ashtrays, all designed by the owners. Ksar Char-Bagh offers its guests unparalleled comfort and service in romantic and select surroundings – not to mention some of the best food in Marrakech (see EAT).

Style 10, Atmosphere 9, Location 7

La Maison Arabe, 1 Derb Assehbe, Bab Doukkala, Medina

Tel: 0 24 38 70 10 www.lamaisonarabe.com
Rates: 1,500–6,000dh

La Maison Arabe was initially opened 60 years ago as a restaurant by two French ladies and became a popular haunt for the likes of Winston Churchill. Having closed in 1983, it was reopened a few years ago as a luxu-

ry hotel by an Italian prince, Fabrizio Ruspoli. The 17 rooms are built around two flower-filled patios and contain a host of modern conveniences, from air-conditioning and telephones to televisions, that find a place amid the more traditional décor (*zellije* bathrooms, fire-

places, private terraces). Built using mostly local methods and materials, the hotel has successfully retained some of the nostalgic charm of a bygone era, although the rooms possess a more corporate aesthetic: think decorative *gebs* and *bejmat* floor-tiling alongside leather desks and minibars. In accordance with the pristine setting, the staff can be overly formal but the facilities – suave Moroccan restaurant, *hammam*, massive pool, cooking school, etc. – and the service more than make up for it.

Style 8, Atmosphere 7, Location 8

Maison Mnabha, 32–33 Derb Mnabha, Kasbah, Medina
Tel: 0 24 38 13 25 www.maisonmnabha.com
Rates: 900–1,300dh

Maison Mnabha is operated by English half-brothers Peter Dyer and Lawrence Brady. They have occupied the house for a decade, but three years ago decided to open it up to the public as a guesthouse. The biggest attraction is the reception area, part of an old 17th-century palace that boasts

original architecture complete with carved wood, calligraphic plasterwork and painted pillars and ceilings. The appeal of the house – or at least of the downstairs – is one of royal refinement; the upstairs area, which is brand new, has a much more modern, breezier feel, containing four main bedrooms and private and public roof terraces. The rooms are not large, but they are modern and comfortable, and with their complementary mix of south-east Asian décor – Buddha heads from Thailand, silks from Laos – and Moroccan ornamentation, are good value for money. The main terrace has great views over the Kasbah, Les Jardins Agdal and the Bahia Palace. Peter rather handily has a PhD on the Kasbah and is a fountain of local knowledge. Snacks and dinner are made to order, a digital television offers programmes in English and WiFi connection keeps you in touch with the rest of the world if necessary.

Style 7, Atmosphere 7, Location 8

La Mamounia, Avenue Bab Jedid, Medina

Tel: 0 24 44 44 09 www.mamounia.com
Rates: 2,850–30,000dh

There's not much to say about the legendary Mamounia hotel that hasn't already been said — apart from saying that much of what has been said is true. Yes, it's the most well-known and most opulent location in all of Marrakesh. Yes, it has put up a host of world-famous guests ranging from the

Prince of Wales to Mick Jagger. Architects Prost and Marchisio, who fused Moroccan architecture with the predominant Art Deco style of the era, built the place in 1922. It was renovated in 1986 but the fusion remains intact, resulting in an old-fashioned and elegant hotel that still gives off an air of refinement and luxury to the 'right' people — and of unnecessary haughtiness to the 'wrong' ones. There are 171 rooms, 57 suites and three separate, exclusive villas, which are all as comfortable and thoroughly equipped as you might expect. As well as the sleeping quarters, there is a whole other Mamounia-world to explore, complete with amusement arcades, gardens, casino, several bars, swimming pool, spa, tennis and squash courts, boutiques and five restaurants. Currently being refurbished La Mamounia reopens in the spring of 2007 with new rooms and an impressive spa.

Style 7, Atmosphere 6, Location 8

Palais Rhoul, Route de Fes, Dar Tounsi, Palmeraie
Tel: 0 24 32 94 94/95 www.palaisrhoul.com
Rates: 2,500–4,900

Owned and managed by a bona fide member of the Rhoul family, this former family home has been frequented by the French jet-set for the last few years, but has recently become a major destination for other monied Europeans. The grandeur implicit in the venue's name is immediately manifest as you traverse the Palais' expansive grounds: a dramatic main hall with

a 40-foot ceiling and an abundance of antique furniture; a grandiloquent circular pool surrounded by patios and rooms; a tented VIP 'village', available only to rent in its entirety and dramatically endowed with African-style furnishings; and a spa and *hammam* (see PLAY) that are arguably the finest in Marrakech. Four of the eight bedrooms and three suites (all have bathrooms and mod-cons such as stereos and fridges) are set around the round pool, while the other four rooms overlook the garden. Each room is decorated with antique furniture and *objets d'art* from around the world, creating an ambience of refined luxury very much in keeping with the rest of the place. There are two restaurants in the complex, one serving good Moroccan cuisine, and another – L'Abyssin (open April to December) – that serves up classy international fare (see EAT). In addition, guests can access a fitness centre, a library/plasma-screen room, cigar room and boutique. And did we mention you can hire a private plane for guest excursions?

Style 9, Atmosphere 9, Location 7

La Pause, Douar Lmih Laroussiere, Commune Agafay

Tel: 0 61 30 64 94 www.lapause-marrakech.com
Rates: 650–1,000dh

Built by eco-friendly Frenchman Frederic Alaime, La Pause is a surreal but idyllic vision nestled in the reasonably remote Agafay desert, around a 45-minute drive from town. Alaime has lovingly constructed a series of traditional Berber-style *pise* buildings – tents, huts, even a *hammam* – that blend in mellifluously with the rolling landscape that surrounds La Pause. Rather than refined luxury, guests can expect a down-to-earth simplicity, coupled with surroundings that exude a sense of quite extraordinary quietude. There's a range of things to do, from a round of crazy golf along a river bed to horse-riding, trekking and cycling. It's an ideal spot for a day trip, but staying overnight allows you fully to absorb the strange beauty of the place –

observing the night stars with zero light pollution, indulging in the fantastic home-made food (with ingredients grown in the organic garden), and sleeping in a house built from natural mud and straw or in one of the cosy tents. A huge bonus with La Pause is that whether you're booking for two or 20, your reservation guarantees you the whole place, enabling you to enjoy the experience with no distractions.

Style 8, Atmosphere 10, Location 7

Riad 12, 12 Derb Sraghnas, Dar el Bacha, Medina

Tel: 0 24 38 76 29 www.uovo.com
Rates: 760–2,100dh

A sister hotel to Riad 72 (see below), Riad 12 has been set up under the auspices of a new umbrella company called Uovo, which is also about to house yet another property in the Medina called Riad Due ('two' in Italian). Though explicitly connected to 72, Riad 12 is distinctly different. It has the same structure, of course, but instead of possessing a strong designer character, this place is light and breezy with a simple but attractive square courtyard, a small pool, whitewashed walls, a notable lack of cluttersome knick-knacks and an overall aura of humble quietude. The names of the rooms – Camellia, Rania and Ines – well reflect the feeling of homely insouciance that is pervasive here. Camillia and Rania are both large (deluxe doubles), and Ines is a smaller single. The rooms are also simply decorated but contain

everything you need, and the discreet service helps to make the place feel more like a private house than a hotel. A very charming location indeed; perfect for singles, couples, or even a small group looking to hire an intimate *riad* all to themselves.

Style 8, Atmosphere 8, Location 8

Riad 72, 72 Arset Awzel, Dar el Bacha, Medina
Tel: 0 24 38 76 29 www.ouvo.com
Rates: 1,200–3,250dh

Constructed around an ultra-relaxing courtyard, Riad 72 is small but perfectly formed. The owner, a Milanese photographer named Giovanna, has a
great sense of style that puts an Italian twist on traditional Moroccan décor
to create a cool, funky and luxurious environment. The four rooms vary in
size dramatically and contain artistically designed beds, but all have gorgeous
bathrooms with basins made from barrels and beaten copper, and differently

coloured *tadelakt* walls. The main suite is the largest room and has the
bonus of a wonderful built-in sunlight. This makes the room next door seem

small, although in
actual fact it is a
perfectly reason-
able size and has an
en-suite bathroom
to die for (and at
half the price of the
bigger room, it is
well worth the
money). Riad 72 is
slightly taller than
most, affording
great views from the attractively attired roof terrace. There's a *hammam* for
guests, and the service and ambience are superbly intimate.

Style 8, Atmosphere 8, Location 8

Riad Azzar, 94 Derb Moulay, Abdelkader, Derb Dabachi, Medina
Tel: 0 61 15 81 73   www.riadazzar.com
Rates: 1,200–2,500dh

Riad Azzar has not been open as long as many of the other *riads* in town,
but it has already made a significant mark. An atmosphere of refined charm
is apparent as soon as you duck into the small entrance and enter an

elegant courtyard area with a gorgeous pool and a homely ambience. There's something immediately affable about the place, and it's a feeling that also pervades the six rooms (three suites, two doubles, one twin) and the other public areas, such as the pleasant alcoves, dining area and roof terrace. While there's nothing outrageously exceptional about the décor in general, everything smacks of a subtle sensuality and a refined taste. The rooms are lovely and teeming with features, from Algerian wardrobes to marble and *tadelakt* bathrooms and private terraces, and all six give off a satisfying, well-manicured air. Sociable owners Cees and Maryk (from Holland) are on site most of the time to give full attention to their guests, and there's great home cooking, and bodycare treatments and massage on offer.

Style 8, Atmosphere 8, Location 8

Riad El Fenn, 2 Derb Moulay Abdallah Ben Hezzian, Bab El Ksour, Medina

Tel: 0 24 44 12 10 www.riadelfenn.com
Rates: 3,500–5,500dh

Vanessa Branson's ultra-chic Medina *riad* has fast become one of the most talked about in Marrakech. Situated at the edge of the Medina, close to the Bab El Ksour, the space has been designed as part family home, part artistic retreat and part commercial business. The 11 rooms and suites are arranged around a typically elegant courtyard, while elsewhere in the deceptively large building are two heated swimming pools, a massage and *hammam* centre, a home cinema (with 10-foot screen), an organic garden, kitchen for

cooking lessons, and WiFi internet throughout. The interior is unusual: simple *tadelakt* rooms presented in turquoise blues, deep reds and simple creams, with assorted decorative features that vary from Murano chandeliers picked up in the Portobello Road to works by acclaimed international artists such as Bridget Riley, Terry Frost and Fiona Rae. The combination results in a creative and stimulating environment with emphasis on comfort and style, provided by consummate hosts/managers Frederic Scholl and Viviana Gonzalez. Together they have ensured the place a Condé Nast hotlist rating as well as a glut of other well-deserved accolades.

Style 9, Atmosphere 9, Location 9

Riad El Mezouar, 28 Derb El Hamman, Issebtinne, Medina.
Tel: 0 24 38 09 49 www.mezouar.com
Rates: 1,900–2,200dh

Located near the Ben Youssef Medersa, the delightful and stylish El Mezouar is the creation of young French architects/designers Jérôme Vermelin and Michel Durand-Meyrier. It used to be an 18th-century palace, 'Mezouar' being the official title bestowed on the branch of the Alaoui royal family

who used to own it. The present owners have worked hard to maintain something of its original feel, especially around the courtyard, which has a traditional-style pool, aromatic garden with jasmine, myrtle, laurel and white roses, plus Arabo–Andalucian arcades and galleries. There are five rooms, which are designed to emphasize the natural spaces and contours of the building: rather than cramming them full of features, the owners have settled on a policy of quality over quantity. Their own designs feature here and there (there's a boutique upstairs) among imported Chinese, Byzantine and Tibetan ornamentation. Food (French and Moroccan) is available on the premises – 200dh lunch, 400dh dinner – made by an excellent local chef, and can be taken in the Moorish alcoves, the grand salons, the courtyard or the terrace. WiFi access and satellite TV are also available.

Style 8, Atmosphere 8, Location 7

Riad Enija, 9 Derb Mesfioui, Rahba Lakdima, Medina
Tel: 0 24 44 09 26 www.riadenija.com
Rates: 2,350–3,500dh (closed July)

Swedish architect Bjorn Conerdings and Swiss designer Ursula Haldimann have transformed this 200-year-old silk-trader's townhouse (around three-quarters of it is still intact) into a living, breathing work of art. The pair collect far-out contemporary pieces, and juxtapose their personal mementos

against more traditional decorative touches. Hence the 12 suites – which have names such as 'Lion', 'Chameleon' and 'Prince' – are kitted out with sculpted wrought-iron four-poster beds, silk floor cushions, Chantal Saccomanno tables and Alain Girel/Mark Brazer mirrors. It can all be a little overwhelming at times, but care has been taken to ensure the more riotous ensembles are balanced by calmer rooms and spaces, adding up to a charmingly eccentric and unique atmosphere. In addition to the rooms, there's a terrace, a jungle of a courtyard, a beauty parlour, a Moroccan kitchen and a large public salon – all of which are maintained by a troupe of 14 girls who float around in elegant red outfits. Two new Indian-themed rooms are expected in 2007.

Style 9, Atmosphere 8, Location 8

Riad Farnatchi, 2 Derb Farnatchi, Qua'at Benahid, Medina
Tel: 0 24 38 49 10 www.riadfarnatchi.com
Rates: 3,100–4,800dh

This exquisitely decorated *riad* opened in March 2004. Originally designed as the home of Jonathan Wix, the man behind The Scotsman in Edinburgh and Hotel de la Tremoille in Paris, Riad Farnatchi has instantly become part of Marrakech's elite accommodation. The renovation took two years to complete, culminating in a stylish fusion of modern European and traditional

Marrakchi design. Designed around two courtyards, the five suites are simple and elegant, affording guests the necessary intimacy as well as the comfort associated with Jonathan's other hotels. Tucked away in the narrow alleyways north of the souks, Farnatchi is not the easiest *riad* to find – and don't even think about trying to reach it by car – but once you're inside the service is mysteriously good, with staff seemingly invisible until the moment you need them. Rooms are ultra-stylish and highly sensual, and come equipped with trimmings such as Bose docks and digital TV, elegant desks, funky showers, chic furnishings and immaculate detailing throughout. There are four new suites coming in 2007 as well as new treatment rooms for the intimate spa. Farnatchi also offers what is arguably one of the best breakfasts in Marrakech.

Style 9, Atmosphere 8, Location 8

Riad Ifoulki, 11 Derb Moqqadem, Arset Loghzail, Medina
Tel: 0 24 38 56 56 www.riadifoulki.com
Rates: 1,000–3,000dh

Ifoulki's attraction lies in its continued resistance to the 'designer *riad*' boom that has assailed Marrakech since the late 1990s. While many have been busy transforming their locales into *Vogue*-esque visions of contemporary cool, Danish owner Peter Bergmann and son have kept Ifoulki's atmosphere distinctly traditional. This means that the space, which is made up several royal houses, has a fairly austere quality, but the advantage is, of course, a much greater sense of authenticity, not to mention larger rooms. The main courtyard especially – a grand old place full of jasmine, olive and orange trees – has impressively big dimensions, while the rooms that run around it

are correspondingly large. The place carries a sophisticated and discreet air, enhanced by the presence of the Bergmanns (who speak ten languages between them) and by such touches as a well-stocked multilingual library, a marble spa (with male and female masseuses), musical and cultural evenings, *tadelakt* and calligraphy courses, a broad selection of fine antiques and an atmosphere of refined congeniality, which all make the place part palace, part cultural centre. Its broad appeal extends to holidaying families, celebrities and foreign diplomats alike.

Style 7, Atmosphere 8, Location 8

Riad Kaiss, 65 Derb Jedid (off Riad Zitoune El Kedim), Medina

Tel: 0 24 44 01 41   www.riadkaiss.com
Rates: 1,470–2,690dh

It took three years to transform Kaiss from a local *riad* (dating from 1860) into the fine guest-house it is now. Owned and constructed by architect Christian Ferre (who still lives here), it's a sizeable place centred around two large courtyards, which, along with  the rooms, are enhanced with a considered amalgam of antiques, Art Deco furnishings, objects from Thailand and a plethora of neatly arranged artistic bits and bobs. The eight rooms all differ décor-wise but are unerring in their quest to seduce romantic souls. The roof is really something to behold: a handsome, florid network of stairways and relaxation areas with a natty plunge pool tucked away discreetly in one corner. The staff can be aloof but the level of service seems more than decent. Other facilities include a fitness room, *hammam* and meals cooked to order on the premises.

Style 7, Atmosphere 7, Location 8

Riad Kniza, 34 Derb l'Hotel, Bab Doukkala, Medina
Tel: 212 24 37 69 42   www.riadkniza.com
Rates: 1,400–3,350dh

Riad Kniza, marketed as an upscale luxury Hotel de Charme, is a traditional building restored by one Mr Bouskri, a man whose impressive 35 years working as a tour guide (see PLAY) has included giving personal tours to the likes of Richard Nixon, Kofi Annan and Brad Pitt. Given Bouskri's slick interpersonal skills, it's no wonder that Kniza prides itself on its hospitality, not to mention its home-from-home atmosphere – no small feat in a place that's kitted out like a mini palace. The styling and décor is 100% Moroccan, with gorgeous fireplaces, traditional furniture and museum-quality antiques (contributed by Mrs Bouskri, who owns one of the most renowned antique shops in the city). It's impeccably done – not too over the top, not too understated – and leans just far enough towards the corporate in the rooms (three deluxe, three royal suites, a duplex suite) to make them very

amenable to business travellers as well as holiday-makers looking for a genuine Moroccan experience. Each room has satellite TV, there is wireless internet available and the home cooking – traditional Moroccan, natch – is some of the best in town.

Style 7, Atmosphere 8, Location 9

Riad Lotus Ambre, 22 Fhal Zefriti, Quartier Ksour, Medina
Tel: 0 24 44 14 05 www.riadslotus.com
Rates: 1,300–2,450dh

At first glance, and in contrast to its sexy sister, Riad Lotus Perle, Riad Lotus Ambre seems to offer a more traditional, Moroccan-themed retreat from the hustle and bustle of the souks and the Medina in general. As traditional

as it seems on the surface, however, with its seductive light-coloured alcoves and peaceful courtyard, the place subtly pops and fizzes with a range of mod-cons, especially in the bedrooms. Stepping into a bedroom is to be transported into a highly swish and thoroughly modern space, where paintings of prominent figures such as Napoleon Bonaparte, Goethe, Chairman Mao or Marilyn Monroe hang on the walls, Bang & Olufsen systems cater for your audio-visual needs and internet access connects you to the outside world – if, of course, you need it. Up on the roof terrace a lush *hammam* and jacuzzi form part of one of the most enjoyable roof-top environments in the city. Style aficionados and homely folk alike won't fail to find Ambre an impressive choice.

Style 9, Atmosphere, Location 8

Riad Lotus Perle, 22 Fhal Zefriti Quartier Ksour, Medina
Tel: 0 24 44 14 05 www.riadslotus.com
Rates: 2,250–2,650

If it's not the sexiest *riad* in the Medina, then Riad Perle Lotus is certainly the bling-est. The traditional *riad* structure – rooms arranged around a central courtyard/garden – is about the only Moroccan part still standing after

designer Antoine Van Doorne stepped in and audaciously transformed the place into an unapologetically ultra-contemporary space that's been described as '*Vogue*-meets-*Miami-Vice*'. The first jaw-slackener is a seven-metre mirror that extends from the heated jacuzzi in the courtyard up to the roof terrace, literally reflecting the *riad*'s distinctively retro-modern black-and-white decorative theme – which stays just about this side of the cheese line. If first impressions are seductive, wait until you see the rooms – raised beds, sequinned carpets, split-level baths, and a host of iconic characters on the walls from Coco Chanel and Newton to Cartier and Gatsby. There's a swimming pool in the courtyard, a Jacuzzi on the roof, a *hammam* and a mini-spa. Each room is equipped with a Bang & Olufsen plasma screen and music system, DVD player, satellite, WiFi and air conditioning, helping to complete the triumph of modernism over tradition.

Style 9, Atmosphere 8, Location 8

Riad Lotus Privilege, Derb Sidi Ali Ben Hamdouch No 69, Medina
Tel: 0 24 44 14 05 www.riadslotus.com
Price: 2,600-5,500dh

Not content with stepping up the riad game in Marrakech with Perle and Ambre (see pages 56 and 57), the Riad Lotus chain now present the even more extravagant Privilege. Architect/designer Antoine Von Doorne has come up trumps again with a coolly contemporary wonderland of shapes,

curves and mod cons. Despite the sizeable dimensions of the place – it's made up of three interconnecting *riads* – there are just five suites. But what suites they are. Much larger than the rooms at the other Lotus places, they offer a similar one-off retro aesthetic and host of technological trimmings (the state of the art Bang & Olfusen multisystem in each room for example). The main suites (downstairs) have ceilings that stretch up seven metres and hide cinema screens that slide down to eye level at the press of a button. The courtyard is wonderfully frondescent and boasts a heated swimming pool as well as a large restaurant that caters for all Lotus guests at lunchtimes and – more controversially – the general public in the evening. There's also a *hammam* and spa on site.

Style 9, Atmosphere 8, Location 8

Riad Mabrouka, 56 Derb El Bahia (off Riad Zitoun El Jedid), Medina

Tel: 0 24 37 75 79 www.riad-mabrouka.com
Rates: 1,400–1,800dh

Riad Mabrouka is named after Mabrouka Bent Salem Bouida, the grandmother of previous owner Catherine Neri, who opened this place as a tribute to her. Those who like the idea of balancing Zen-styled interiors with funky minimalist furnishings should not hesitate to seek it out. Built by architect Christophe Simeon and run by manager Philippe, it displays a cool and tastefully  restrained artfulness. Wooden furnishings, white walls, a beautiful courtyard with a trickling show-pool, antique packing trunks and *tadelakt* bathrooms are balanced against a seductive savannah backdrop of greys, whites and browns, all repeated in strategically placed giant mirrors. The two suites and three double rooms are similarly delightful, although they walk the tightrope between cosy and small. There are salons downstairs for relaxing in, a lovely roof terrace and traditional Moroccan food is available on order. The Musée de Marrakech is nearby.

Style 8, Atmosphere 8, Location 8

Riad Mehdi, 2 Derb Sedra, Bab Agnaou, Medina
Tel: 0 24 38 47 13   www.riadmehdi.net
Rates: 1,400–2,600dh

With four suites (including a duplex apartment-style chamber) and five standard double rooms, an extensive spa and *hammam* complex next door, and a good location just inside the Bab Agnaou gate, Riad Mehdi is an attractive proposition all round. The usual runs of smooth *tadelakt* walls, *zellije* tiling and *bejmat* floors are found throughout, although since it was built from scratch three years ago, a certain feeling of modernity creeps through the décor. Rooms aren't as large as they could be but they are certainly adequate, and  decorated unostentatiously with comfort and sensuality rather than hipness in mind. The outside courtyard backs onto the ancient Medina walls. It's a divine little hideaway with a regulated-temperature pool, a bar just inside the main doors and even a small dining area. If you want a holiday packed with relaxation, health and beauty then this could well be the right place for you (see PLAY).

Style 7, Atmosphere 7, Location 8

Riad Tchaikana, 25 Derb El Ferrane, Kaat Benahid, Medina
Tel: 0 24 38 51 50   www.tchaikana.com
Rates: 800–1,500dh

Run by ultra-hospitable Belgian couple Delphine and Jean-François, Tchaikana is simply one of the best value-for-money *riads* in the Medina. Delphine used to jaunt around Africa looking for artefacts and crafts to trade in the art store she had in Brussels before moving here. Now her collection creates a tasteful sub-Saharan theme throughout this slickly minimal-

ist haven of tranquillity. Wall hangings, furnishings and ornamentation are strewn carefully across a backdrop of restrained browns and beiges in rooms as big as suites, and suites that could double as aircraft hangars. The bathrooms are features in their own right, voluptuous and rustic with beautiful touches such as *tadelakt* basins. Downstairs, much of the original 19th-century design has been kept intact (stucco detailing, cedarwood doors), and surrounds a romantic courtyard overlooked by orange and citrus trees and enclosed by rooms and salons. There's WiFi access and a wide range of music and books, and the owners are relaxed, hip and very knowledgeable about local culture, making this a great option for style-conscious travellers.

Style 8, Atmosphere 8, Location 8

Riad Tizwa, 26 Derb Gueraba, Dar El Bacha, Medina
Tel: 0 68 88 13 47 www.riadtizwa.co.uk
Price: 1,450dh

Located a short mooch from the Galoui's Palace at Dar El Bacha along the Rue Larous, Riad Tizwa is the creation of Englishman Richard Bee who, inspired by a stay at Riad El Fenn (see page ?) decided to open his own guest house. Tizwa doesn't borrow too much from the El Fenn aesthetic however, settling on a much more traditional design ethic complete with *zellije* tiles and colourful stucco, though it does share El Fenn's feeling of intimacy. In fact even more so, since you don't book individual rooms here: it's the lot or nothing. Of the five rooms, only two of them are en suite and the downstairs room is decidedly poky (it's listed as a double but would be

more suitable as a single), but the rest are perfectly sizeable and all are decorated with homely rugs and pleasantly coloured runs of *tadelakt* in the rooms and bathrooms. There are several pleasant salons, a cracking roof terrace and savvy touches like iPod docking stations and Haviana flip flops. Naturally, a member of staff is on hand at all times to cook and clean and cater for your very whim. Itineraries can also be tailor-made by the owner.

Style 7, Atmosphere 8, Location 8

Riad W, Derb Boutouil No 41, Kennaria, Medina
Tel: 0 65 36 79 36 www.riadw.com
Rates: 900–1,500dh

Compact and immaculately presented, Riad W is a brand-spanking new addition to Marrakech's glut of *riads*. Managed by hospitable Frenchwoman Elsa, W consists of just four rooms, each one a different shape, style and price.

Although Elsa doesn't have a background in interior design, she has great taste and a way of making spaces feel contemporary yet homely: low wooden tables with woollen seat covers, modern plastic chairs in traditional courtyard spaces; L-shaped pool; elongated brick fireplaces. The chic-cum-cosy aesthetic extends to all the rooms, where large beds rest on raised floors, fireplaces hug the walls and the shower rooms are adorable. The décor is smart and new throughout, and always pleasing to the eye; and although the smallest room is very small, it is correspondingly priced. The other rooms are all decent sizes, and the biggest one has a large roof window for extra light. All in all, W offers unbeatable contemporary charm at very decent prices.

Style 8, Atmosphere 7, Location 8

Riyad El Cadi, 87 Derb Moulay Abdelkader, Dabachi, Medina
Tel: 0 24 37 86 55   www.riyadelcadi.com
Rates: 1,200–3,000dh

Part *maison d'hôte*, part museum, El Cadi is famous for its stunning collection of rare antiquities and textiles, the personal property of late owner, the former German ambassador Herwig Bartels. The Riad El Cadi – now run by his

amiable daughter Julia – dates back to the 13th and 14th centuries, making it much older than many others in the Medina. The winding staircases and twisting corridors connect six houses, all of which still bear separate names and identities and can be rented out in their entirety. The place is a maze of patios, salons and passages to the suites and rooms, which all differ in size, décor and layout (and also in price), although all have their own private bathrooms (the four rooms on the ground floor have showers; those on the first floor have baths). The impeccably tasteful decoration (ancient Berber costumes, antique textiles from the Atlas, Ottoman embroideries) extends throughout the public areas and all the rooms, and the service is both highly discreet and superbly efficient. El Cadi also boasts a swimming pool, a jacuzzi, a *hammam*, a well-stocked library, large terraces, dining and conference rooms, plus wifi in the courtyard, massages on demand, and a wonderful range of Bordeaux wines.

Style 8, Atmosphere 8, Location 8

Ryad Dyor, I Derb Driba Jdida, Sidi Ben Slimane, Medina
Tel: 0 24 37 59 80 www.ryaddyor.com
Rates: 1,280–2950dh

Riad Dyor opened just under a year ago but has fast become one of the more established places to stay. Designed by Yvonna Hulst and Alberto Cortes (who have already transformed eight luxury villas in Ibiza) and run by relaxed Dutch manager Paul Levieveld, the *riad* – or rather the two adjoining *riads*, which have been merged to create a mini-labyrinth – adhere to a spirited aesthetic of high-end eclecticism. Moroccan textiles and fittings

are interspersed with Timney Fowler cushions, Perspex chairs and other furnishings, both funky and formal, from Europe, Asia and North Africa. There are five suites and two double rooms, all of which are uniquely deco-

rated and on the spacious side, with double beds, *tadelakt* bathrooms, fireplaces, desks and chairs. A mosaic-tiled courtyard offers some pleasant lounging areas, and there's a plunge pool and a roof terrace that affords good views of the Medina. The only drag about Dyor is that, compared with many *riads*, it's a little out of the way, and there's not so much going on in this part of the Medina. That said, it's really only a short walk to the action, and many might prefer the relative scarcity of tourists around this neighbourhood. Manager Paul works hard to ensure that nothing is lacking during any stay here.

Style 8, Atmosphere 8, Location 7

La Sultana, rue de la Kasbah, Kasbah, Medina
Tel: 0 24 38 80 08   www.lasultanamarakech.com
Rates: 2,560–9,530dh

La Sultana opened its doors to the public in the spring of 2004, immediately becoming a member of Small Luxury Hotels Of The World, though 'small' isn't the first adjective that leaps to mind when you step inside the grandiose door into what would appear to be an opulent palace of a place. Located just off a main thoroughfare in the Kasbah and overlooking the Saadian Tombs, the building took three years to reassemble, and required experienced local craftsmen to reconstruct the classical Moroccan architecture. There are 21 rooms, arranged over three levels, and around four separate courtyards that display a range of different artisan's materials (*tadelakt*, wood, brick, paint). More hotel-like that many other *riads*, Sultana offers an impressive array of traditional and modern extras – there are giant giraffe paintings in the rooms alongside DVD players and ADSL points (no wireless). The roof terrace incorporates an open-air massage centre and a quiet space for drinks at sunset, while downstairs a swimming pool set in a verdant courtyard helps ease the heat of the day and a small, ship-themed bar (complete with underwater views of the pool) is well stocked. The restaurant, which serves a mix of delicious Moroccan cuisine and international food, is open to the public (see EAT).

Style 8, Atmosphere 8, Location 8

Tigmi, Route d'Amizmiz, Douar Tagadert, Ait el kadi Tamslouht
Tel: 0 24 48 40 20 ww.tigmi.com
Rates: 1,280–2,640dh

Where Caravanserai (see page 32) is located in a rural Arabic village, Tigmi is ensconced within a Berber village ('*tigmi*' means 'house' in Berber) and is set even further out of the city (it's a good 30-minute drive). The village in question, Tagadert, is set in the rolling foothills of the High Atlas Mountains

and overlooks a verdant, picturesque valley, complete with river and hills. Tigmi was designed, built and owned until recently by Englishman Max Lawrence, and his distinctive touch is evident through subtle dreamtime architecture infused with an incredible sense of calm and rustic mystique. The entire reconstruction work was carried out using only local materials, with thousands of new bricks made from the sifted earth, mixed with straw and water, which was dug out of the ground to make the large pool. The 10

66

suites are all showpieces in themselves, managing to combine the vividly exotic with an otherworldly charm. Most of them have separate bedrooms, sitting rooms and bathrooms, and most also have fireplaces for the winter evening chill. All the rooms have en-suite bathrooms with showers (no baths). Amenities include a secluded TV room, pool, restaurant, a small gym, *hammam*, gardens and roof terraces with 360-degree views of the surrounding countryside. Cycles are also available for local excursions.

Style 9, Atmosphere 9, Location 7

Toubkal Trekking Lodge, Id Issa, Azzaden valley, Atlas Massif
Tel: 0 24 48 56 11 www.kasbahdutoubkal.com
Rates: 2,000dh

The latest project of the well-established Atlas address Kasbah Du Toubkal, this trekking lodge was built a year or so ago to cater for the growing number of trekkers requesting a good standard of accommodation deeper in the mountains. Set in the dramatic Azzaden valley in the Toubkal Massif, this remote lodge has been constructed in a very similar way to the Kasbah (see page 41). Built in a traditional style from local, eco-friendly materials, the lodge boasts Berber features such as wooden ceilings and carved doors, and a plethora of creature comforts: solar-powered underfloor heating, a wonderful terrace, wood-burning stove and en-suite bathrooms in all three rooms. Needless to say the place affords spectacular views across the valley. It takes a half or full day to get here from the Kasbah du Toubkal, depending

on your route and mode of travel (foot, bicycle, donkey, horse, car) but once here you can use it as a stopover point, or as a base to undertake shorter walks in the surrounding area.

Style 8, Atmosphere 10, Location 7

Villa Des Orangers, 6 rue Sidi Mimoun, Place Ben Tachfine, Medina

Tel: 0 24 38 46 38 www.villadesorangers.com
Rates: 3,200–7,000dh

Blink and you'll miss the unassuming entrance to this Relais & Chateaux member – one of the most highly regarded *riads* in town. Right on the bustling rue Sidi Mimoun, close to the Jemaa el Fna, and overlooking the Koutoubia Mosque, its location is unlikely, yet convenient. Once inside the doors, the heat and sweat of the outside world drifts away and your senses feast instead on the water channels full of floating rose petals, orange-treed courtyard, alcoves full of soft sofas and gently gurgling fountains. The 19 rooms and suites are all spacious and stylish, with a sense of gentle sophis-

tication, and the atmosphere is generally low-key, making it a major draw for well-to-do Europeans and the odd celebrity. The recent opening of a new courtyard means there is now a good-size pool on the ground floor as well as on the roof terrace, a massage centre, boutique and three extra suites.

Style 8, Atmosphere 8, Location 9

Villas of Morocco, 37 Lowndes Square, London, SW1
Tel: +44 207 823 0999 www.villasofmorocco.com

Villas of Morocco offer an excellent range of high end luxury villas for private rentals. Scattered around Morocco, but predominantly found in the Marrakech region, the villas offer wonderfully luxuriant settings and an impressive level of service. The beautiful villas, often simply private houses occasionally rented out, they will cater from a small party of four or five to a full-blown house party of 18. Founded a couple of years ago, the properties on offer are comfortable, discreet, and above all, charming. Offering butlers and a in-house concierge service they

can arrange anything from a round of golf for two to a full-blown party for 200. Catering to many of the major 'A' list celebrities who visit the country, Villas of Morocco are the leaders in the private villa market.

Style 9, Atmosphere 9, Location 9

eat...

It's no coincidence there's a lack of weighing scales in Marrakech. Eating is one of the primary experiences of being here, and the classic Moroccan table isn't shy about serving up banquets fit for an oriental king or queen. Checking your weight in the midst of such feeding frenzies would only serve to spoil your holiday.

Despite its reputation as a place for over-the-top gastronomic experiences, dining in Marrakech these days is a surprisingly diverse and delightful experience. The last few years have seen a rise in chic, international restaurants – mainly French and Italian, with an increasingly large selection of Asian – that compete with the traditional Moroccan hotspots to create an impressive range of options.

First of all, though, the classic Moroccan feast. This phenomenon usually takes place at what are known colloquially as 'palace' restaurants, so-called because they are often renovated 18th- or 19th-century palaces or royal buildings. The décor is classic Moroccan; waiters wear traditional attire; fountains gurgle; tables are strewn with rose petals; exotic (belly) dancers wiggle in front of you and consecutive plates of food are brought to your table – all for a fixed fee – until you are forced to accept defeat, gasping 'no more, no more'. Then they bring dessert.

The ritual usually begins with a platter of hors d'oeuvres or *briouettes* (deep-fried envelopes of filo pastry containing anything from ground meat to cheese), followed by a *pastilla* (a larger and sweeter wrap of filo pastry containing chicken or pigeon, cooked with almonds, spices, cinnamon and sugar), and then a couple of main courses: a *tajine* (a stew of meat and/or vegetables cooked with spices and fruit and served in conical dishes) and couscous (ground semolina flour served with meat and/or vegetables), followed by anything between one and three different desserts. The best places to sample this quintessential experience are Marjana and Tobsil. Thankfully there are à la carte options for Moroccan food too – El Fassia is the best, followed closely by the superb Dar Moha.

As a general rule the more modern restaurants are situated in Gueliz or further outside the city. Venues such as Jad Mahal, Le Comptoir and Bô-Zin are all places to be seen in as much as eat in, although the food is generally of a decent standard too. Less buzzing places – but equally good in terms of food, and often cheaper – include the dark, seductive Lolo Quoi, and the bright and breezy Kech Mara out in Gueliz, or the chic Foundouk in the Medina. If you want seriously good food in unique settings, try Jnane Tamsna, Ksar Char Bagh or the Amanjena, which offers the best Thai food in town by a long way.

Prices and quality, as everywhere, vary. You can pick up a bite on the atmospheric stalls of the Jemaa el Fna for under 50dh, or pay considerably more to eat somewhere incredibly exclusive, although even then you'll rarely pay more than 600–700dh per head. Prices quoted here represent the average cost of a starter and main course for one person, with a glass of wine.

Our top 10 restaurants in Marrakech are:
1. El Fassia
2. Dar Moha
3. Jnane Tamsna
4. Le Tobsil
5. Sur Une Ardoise
6. Ksar Char-Bagh
7. Bô-Zin
8. Hadika
9. Amanjena Thai
10. Jad Mahal

The top 5 for food are:
1. El Fassia
2. Jnane Tamsna
3. Bô-Zin
4. Dar Moha
5. L'Abyssin

The top 5 for service are:
1. Bô-Zin
2. Amanjena Thai
3. El Fassia
4. Sur Une Ardoise
5. Dar Moha

The top 5 for atmosphere are:
1. Jemaa el Fna
2. Bô-Zin
3. Jad Mahal
4. Jnane Tamsna
5. L'Abyssin

L'Abyssin, Palais Rhoul, Route De Fes, Dar Tounsi

Tel: 0 24 32 85 84 www.palais-rhoul.com
Open: 8–11pm. Closed Monday and Tuesday lunch.   450dh
International

L'Abyssin is decidedly the hipper of the two restaurants that belong to the majestic Palais Rhoul (see SLEEP). In fact, the funky design and cooler-than-cool allure couldn't make more of a contrast with the formal elegance of the main hotel. Set in a gorgeous garden area (complete with verbose

frogs), it really is nothing more than a series of white tents arranged in a square around a minimal courtyard. The milky décor, complete with white curtains flapping in the breeze, large, comfy sofas (also white) and low tables create a superb 'lounge' ambience. The tents are exposed to the elements on warm summer days and nights, and buttoned up tight with transparent sheets when it's colder. During the winter the whole area is enclosed in a giant tent and decorated with exotic flowers. The menu isn't hugely extensive but it is interesting and the chefs usually – but not always – create meals that are above average. It's not as expensive as it could be, although anyone staying in the Medina will be adding a 200dh return taxi ride to the bill. A good option might be to use the fabulous Palais Rhoul spa and enjoy dinner here afterwards (see PLAY). Bookings for both are recommended.

Food 7, Service 8, Atmosphere 8

Amanjena Thai, Route de Ouarzazate, Km 12

Tel: 0 24 40 33 53 www.amanresorts.com
Open: 10am–3pm, 7pm–11pm daily   425dh
Thai

The influence of Asian cuisine has slowly been seeping into Marrakech's menus, but no one as yet has managed to make Thai food with the same kind of pedigree as the three chefs who command the Amanjena's Thai

restaurant (The Thai as it's colloquially known). Vital items are flown in especially from Thailand so that dishes really do taste as good here as they do in Bangkok. The best spot to dine (if it's fine) is on the terrace next to the pool. Choose from a reasonably elaborate selection that includes Thai green curry, stir-fried squid, king prawns and salads, or if you're not in the mood for Thai food try the less exotic but still tasty options: sandwiches, gazpacho soup and burgers. There's a great wine list and, weather permitting (usually May to September), tables are also set up near the pool in the evenings. Drawbacks are the cost of a taxi ride out here and back, and the fact you can't use the pool unless you're a guest – it's quite frustrating to watch people splashing around on a hot day after your meal and know you can't join in. Best perhaps to combine a lunch with use of the expensive spa/*hammam* facilities. Reservations are essential.

Food 8, Service 9, Atmosphere 8

Bagatelle, 101 rue Yougoslavie, Gueliz

Tel: 0 24 43 02 74

Open: noon–2.30pm, 7.30–10.30pm. Closed Wednesdays.   170dh

French

Bagatelle is a well-established French-run restaurant located in the centre of
Gueliz. It's been in the same family since 1949, the current owner being the
daughter-in-law of the original patron, while her son now manages the
restaurant. The main, vine-covered doors lead directly off the street and into
two areas. In all but the coldest weather, people head for the attractive outdoor terrace, where grapes dangle through wooden trelliswork above your

head and foliage breathes reassuringly around you. The tried-and-tested
menu isn't particularly extensive, but the food – which consists mainly of
French-style meat and fish dishes with the odd traditional dish (*couscous*,
tajine or *salade Morocaine*) thrown in for good measure – is consistently
good and the staff are relaxed and reliable. For colder weather, there's an
indoor section next door with a couple of fireplaces to banish the winter
chill.

Food 7, Service 8, Atmosphere 8

Bô-Zin, Douar Lohna, Route de l'Ourika 3.5km

Tel: 0 24 38 80 12 www.bo-zin.com

Open: 8pm–1am daily   450dh

International

'Bo', pronouned '*beau*', or 'beautiful' in French, means the same as 'Zin' –

'beautiful' in Arabic. No modesty here then, which is just as well since it's currently the place in Marrakech where beautiful people like to strut their stuff and flaunt their goods, taking over from older dames like Le Comptoir as the place to see and be seen. The restaurant is chic Parisian in style and boasts a comprehensive international menu (French, Italian, Asian,

Moroccan) served in an elegant but laid-back interior. The terrace is particularly pleasant, although it's worth trying to get a spot in the alluring (and surprisingly intimate) garden. Dim lighting and soft music add to the mood, but as the night wears on the tunes gets louder, belly-dancers emerge from nowhere, and it's not unusual to see punters clambering up onto the tables. With great food and an atmosphere and service to match, Bô-Zin is very much worth the trip out of town.

Food 8, Service 9, Atmosphere 9

Le Comptoir, Avenue Rechouada, Gueliz/Hivernage
Tel: 0 24 43 77 02
Open: 4pm–1am (2.30am Fri, Sat) daily   425dh
Moroccan

The sister restaurant of the Parisian Comptoir opened with a dynamic fanfare a few years ago, quickly setting a new standard for restaurants in Marrakech and becoming a key hang-out for the city's A-list clientele. Its grandeur has faded somewhat (largely thanks to newer, more upbeat kids on the block), but it remains a significant spot for first-time tourists wanting exposure to the city's legendary mix of chic and exoticism. The culinary

action takes place in a dark, seductive main room whose suggestive curves
and luxurious reds and blacks are reminiscent of a Far Eastern opium den.
Pretty waitresses float around in pink designer dresses, musicians massage
the ears, and candles illuminate the faces of the local cognoscenti. The menu
is predictably unpredictable and the standard of the food varies quite dramatically, but the culinary experience is, in any case, secondary to the experience of actually being there. After the belly-dancers have whirled around a
few times, follow the sumptuous stairwell up to the bar area or skip outdoors to the garden and enjoy a cocktail while reclining against a silky cush-
ion. Service is patchy and prices are high, but not many places still carry a
buzz like this.

Food 7, Service 7, Atmosphere 9

Crystal, Pacha, Nouvelle Zone Hotelière de 'Aguedal
Tel: 0 24 38 84 80   www.pachamarrakech.com
Open: 8pm–midnight daily   425dh
International

There are two restaurants and a chill-out room attached to the large complex that goes under the umbrella name of Pacha. Of the two, the most
prominent and most interesting is Crystal (the other is Jana, a chic
Moroccan eaterie), which offers a stylish selection of international cuisine in
a plush art-deco environment. It's an immediately attractive place, located
next to the main Pacha pool (the doors open out in the summer), with soft
cream and brown furnishings that invite casual relaxation while maintaining
a fairly exclusive air. The menu is interesting, with a range of international

options and plenty of fish, and the meals, some of which are quite ambitious, do tend to be well executed and are presented by a team headed by a Ducasse-trained chef. The whole operation is pretty slick and of course after your meal you get the option to relax in the extravagant chill out bar or party on down at the main club.

Food 7, Service 8, Atmosphere 8

Dar Marjana, 15 Derb Sidi Ali Tair, Bab Doukkala, Medina
Tel: 0 24 38 51 10/57 73 www.darmarjanamarrakech.com
Open: 8–11pm. Closed Tuesdays,   660dh
Moroccan

Dar Marjana, a family home for almost 100 years, was opened to the public as a restaurant some 23 years ago. The current patron was born here, and

the rest of the family still live on site, although the place feels more like a palace than a home. Guests are led into an exquisite cypress-treed courtyard for an aperitif to be sipped on divans among softly glowing lanterns around the central fountain. At serving time, you are then seated in one of the four salons (arranged on two floors) or the roof terrace, whereupon a deluge of delicious food served on plates the size of dustbin lids and in *tajine* pots as big as circus tents. Quality as well as quantity is evidently the motto here, since the food is of an incomparable standard. The atmosphere becomes generally more convivial as the night goes on. By the time your stomach is at bursting-point and your mind well oiled with fine wine (the fixed price includes unlimited drinks), the music gets louder and a dancer enters the fray, encouraging group participation – a few well-placed notes tucked into her costume are welcome. Seafood and vegetarian dishes are available on request (call ahead) as are special roasted lamb plates at extra cost. Reservations are essential.

Food 8, Service 8, Atmosphere 8

Dar Moha, 81 rue Dar el Bacha, Medina
Tel: 0 24 38 64 00 www.darmoha.ma
Open: noon–3pm, 7.30pm–late. Closed Mondays.   460dh
Moroccan

Moha is named after its owner Mohammed, an extrovert Moroccan chef who lived and worked in Switzerland for 14 years before returning and opening this rather fine restaurant. The venue itself used to be a royal *riad*

(the palace is just across the road) before Moha transformed it into an ultra-romantic establishment that is considered by many to be the premier dining spot in town. It's difficult to argue. A splendid petal-

covered courtyard leads into a spacious room full of large white tables, decorated in refined Moroccan style, with an upstairs that's designed for either group or intimate dining. The best spot, however, is out the back, especially in the evenings, where tables surround a luminescent pool and beautifully romantic setting. The cuisine here – traditional Moroccan with a Moha twist – is almost flawless. Great care has been taken to ensure the food is devoid of unnecessary fat and sugar but still tastes delicious. Not only that but it's also available as à la carte or fixed menu at lunchtimes as well as in the evening.

Food 8, Service 9, Atmosphere 7

Dar Zellij, 1 Kaasour, Sidi Ben Slimane, Medina
Tel: 0 24 38 26 27   www.darzellij.com
Open: 7.30pm–close Wed–Mon; 11am–3pm Sat–Sun. Closed Tuesdays   350dh
Moroccan

Once upon a time Dar Zellij was a guesthouse. In fact, it was one of the first traditional houses to be converted into a *maison d'hote* and was thus partly responsible for kick-starting the whole 'riad' boom' that has infected Marrakech ever since. In contrast with many other 'designer' spots, Zellij was a Spartan affair with 17th-century detailing left nakedly on display rather than being restored by modern artisans. The fine stucco detailing, cedarwood ceilings, decorated doors and eponymous tiling are still the big draw now, even though the place is run as a restaurant. The main courtyard is an appealing blend of whitewashed pillars and walls, and red carpets and rose petals. Aside from the main dining area there's a series of more

intimate alcoves, rooms and patios to dine in, as well as a charming roof terrace where you can enjoy an aperitif. The menu is resolutely Moroccan – *pastilles*, *tajines* and couscous galore – and comes in the shape of a couple of fixed menu options (350dh/400dh), the contents of which morph every month. Arabo–Andalucian music on Fridays and Saturdays makes Zellij a good weekend option, and there's a Moroccan brunch on offer at lunchtime too (weekends only) for a reasonable 180dh per person.

Food 8, Service 8, Atmosphere 8

El Fassia, 232 Avenue Mohammed V, Gueliz.
Tel: 0 24 43 40 60
Open: noon–2.30pm, 7.30–11pm daily   250dh
Moroccan

Owned and run solely by women (apart from the male door staff, natch), El Fassia is a unique proposition in Morocco. A traditional and elegant space, it's well tended by the owners who busy themselves efficaciously, sleeves

rolled up, creating a relaxed atmosphere while always remaining attentive. Large traditional paintings adorn the walls, the silk napkins have been studiously embroidered, and the overall impression is of eating in someone's (somewhat opulent) home. The menu is as traditional as the interior, and has – gasp! – à la carte options (one of the only decent Moroccan restaurants that does) as well as a fixed menu. All the classic dishes are here as well as a few more innovative ones. Call ahead and you can order the exact food you want, although the regular menu provides some of the best local cuisine in town. The outside patio is the best option – make sure you book ahead.

Food 9, Service 9, Atmosphere 8

Le Foundouk, 55 rue du Souk des Fassi, Kat Bennahid, Medina
Tel: 0 24 37 81 90
Open: noon–midnight. Closed Mondays.   300dh
Moroccan

Traditionally, a 'foundouk' was a resting-place for tradesmen passing through town for the night. They would store their wares downstairs (the doors were locked) and get a night's sleep in one of the rooms upstairs. Most of them are now used as artisans' workshops, but this one has been cunningly transformed into a rather dapper restaurant by a pair of French furniture designers. In keeping with the old-style structure, it has three floors of galleries (includ-

ing the ground floor) centred around a courtyard, which serves as a funky pre-drink/snack or lunch spot, with nifty décor and cool music. The first floor is très chic, arranged for intimate dining, while the highlight is the exquisite roof terrace, illuminated by candles at night and offering sweeping views over the Medina. In keeping with the general ambience, the menu is innovative and elegant, with a mix of predominantly French and Italian dishes and traditional staples. With good service, a congenial ambience and decent, reasonably priced food, this is definitely one of Marrakech's hotspots.

Food 8, Service 8, Atmosphere 8

Hadika, Impasse du Moulin, off Avenue Zerktouni, Gueliz

Tel: 0 24 42 30 46
Open: 8pm–1am daily. Closed Mondays.   250dh
Seafood

This brand new restaurant, located opposite the biggest synagogue in Gueliz (next to the well-known *L'ecole American* off Avenue Zerktouni), was set up by a French family inspired by the seafood spots they found while holidaying on the coast of Thailand. Hidden behind tall pink walls, the space has a large Zen garden, an equally capacious indoor dining area and a couple of rooms where you choose your poison from a selection of Moroccan wines, set in open racks, and your *poisson* from an oblong bed of sparkling ice. Aside from

sea bass, St Pierre, dorade and lotte, there are lobsters, oysters, calamari, crayfish and spider-crabs – all of which arrives fresh each day from the coastal spots of Essouira and Safi – plus chargrilled meats such as ribs of beef and lamb chops. There are also a couple of fixed entrées – the *calamari a la plancha* is divine – and sides (rice, wok-fried vegetables), and the option to have your 'catch' served as a *brochette* or a *medallion*. The dessert menu is also good, the garden atmosphere romantic and the service brisk and amiable.

Food 8, Service 8, Atmosphere 8

Le Jacaranda, 32 Boulevard Zerktouni, Gueliz

Tel: 0 24 44 72 15   www.lejacaranda.ma
Open: noon–11pm daily   300dh
French

Le Jacaranda isn't an especially attractive proposition from the outside. The exterior is featureless and the location on the busy '4-Café' intersection along Mohammed V doesn't seem to promise much tranquillity. However, inside is a decidedly charming space with food that surpasses expectations

in both quality and price. Owner/master chef Philippe Coustal (from Toulouse) has had the place for 15 years and has created an amicable interior that blends traditional, elegant overtones with a quiet riot of lightly expressed purples and oranges. The menu boasts splendid French nouvelle cuisine as well as Moroccan and 'international' dishes, and offers the option of set meals or plenty of à la carte choices. There's an extensive wine list of local and European wines, the walls are regularly used to display art exhibitions (which change every six weeks or so), and there is live music at weekends.

Food 7, Service 8, Atmosphere 7

Jad Mahal, Fontaine de la Mamounia, Bab Jedid, Hivernage
Tel: 0 24 43 69 84   palaisjadmahal@menara.ma
Open: 7.30pm–1am daily   400dh
Moroccan

Jad Mahal is part of a new breed of entertainment restaurants that has sprung up in the last couple of years, following a trend begun by the successful Le Comptoir. The emphasis here is on style and atmosphere as opposed to culinary excellence, but that's not to say the food is at all poor. The brainchild of three French fashion designers, this restaurant-cum-bar-

cum-club has
become the venue
of choice for socie-
ty Marrakchi and
wealthier visitors
to town. The
Arabian Indian
décor, languid seat-
ing and exclusive
atmosphere is
home to some fine

Franco–Moroccan cooking. The menu is prepared monthly by Xavier
Mathieu, a Michelin starred chef and would-be Gary Rhodes who visits from
France to discuss the menu with executive chef Vincent Faucher. As the
evening wears on, the wine flows, the music is pumped up, and then to
tumultuous applause some of the finest (and most beautiful) belly-dancers in
Marrakech arrive to liven up proceedings.

Food 8, Service 7, Atmosphere 9

Les Jardins de la Koutoubia, 26 rue de la Koutoubia, Medina
Tel: 0 24 38 88 00   www.lesjardinsdelakoutoubia.com
Open: noon–4pm, 7.30–10.30pm daily   350dh
Moroccan/Spanish

There are three restaurants at the Jardins de la Koutoubia, and all of them
are worth a visit. On the ground floor, just off the reception, is the *restau-*

rant gastronomique, a refined space with an abundance of tables and formal décor that serves a range of sophisticated French dishes. It's a good place to eat if it's relatively busy, but when it's empty its size and starchiness can result in a rather reserved experience. Next door, on the ground floor, is a new Moroccan restaurant that offers a selection of well-prepared local dishes. A more relaxed option in this instance is to head for the more intimate tables that skirt the pool or climb the stairs to the rather romantic Basque restaurant. This looks out over the Koutoubia Mosque and serves wonderful Spanish-influenced food and freshly prepared fish dishes. The price in both places is very reasonable, especially the lunchtime deals downstairs, which can be combined with a dip in the hotel pool if the management is feeling liberal.

Food 8, Service 8, Atmosphere 7

Les Jardins De La Medina, 21 Derb Chtouka, Kasbah
Tel: 0 24 38 18 51   www.lesjardinsdelamedina.com
Open: 12–3pm, 7–11pm daily   250dh
International/Moroccan

The bad news is that Les Jardins… no longer offers previous chef Najiz Hicham Hicham's formidable chocolate-tower desserts; the good news is that his little-known tradition of making Thai food with 24 hours, notice is continued by the new chef, and to the same high standard. The lunch menu here boasts a tasty range of meals and convenient 'snack' options (delicately cooked burgers and sandwiches), while at night, international and Moroccan dishes reign supreme. There are two main eating areas in the hotel: the seating around the pool is casual and more suited to lunchtimes (note that the

pool is strictly reserved for residents), while the inside is slightly more formal and better for evenings or rainy days. We wouldn't recommend going out of your way to dine here at night, but those who find themselves stuck in the fairly quiet Kasbah region could find Les Jardins… a more than civilized lunch-time option.

Food 7, Service 8, Atmosphere 6

Jemaa el Fna
Open: 7–11.30pm daily   75dh
Moroccan

If you're feeling adventurous and want to eat in true 'Marrakchi' style, simply grab a seat at one of the sizzling food stalls in the nocturnal Jemaa el Fna. After dark the place becomes a giant open-air barbecue as locals set up their stalls – illuminated by strings of light-bulbs – and start harassing passers-by to sample their culinary wares. It's a superbly photogenic sight

viewed from an upper terrace of a nearby café or restaurant, but the up-close experience is really something else. There's not a great deal of difference between one stall and another in terms of quality, but some sell things that others don't, and it might be worth eating where the most Moroccans are eating. You can get anything from fried fish, kebabs and salads to a sheep's head, brains or steamed snails. If you want to rejoice in Marrakech's ancient and modern sights and smells, this is the place to do it. However, it may be better to leave it until the end of your stay, just in case!

Food 6, Service 7, Atmosphere 10

Jnane Tamsna, Douar Abiad, Palmeraie

Tel: 0 24 32 93 40

Open: noon–10.30pm daily   300dh lunch/500dh dinner

International

Jnane Tamsna (see SLEEP) is one of the more popular villas out in the Palmaraie, not only because of its seductive architecture and design features, but also because of the vast organic gardens, which lend the place a unique atmosphere of genuine tranquillity. The Tamsna gardens have a practical use too in that they provide many of the ingredients for the kitchen, which

recently opened its doors to the public. In the summer, tables are set outside on a serene stretch of patio next to the main house. There's no menu as such. You are simply seated and attended by elegant waiters, who serve up three sumptuous courses plus wine (for an extra charge) and coffee. The food, customized versions of Mediterranean, French, Moroccan and Senegalese dishes, leans towards the wholesome and nutritious, and is prepared by five different chefs, including three women, an Australian and a former executive chef of Quinta do Lago Four Seasons. It's a trip to get out to Jnane Tamsna, of course, but the unique environment and delicious food make it more than worthwhile, especially at lunchtime when you can also splash around in one of the villa's pools for the afternoon or even use the tennis courts. On colder days and evenings, meals are served inside the house In an equally tranquil and urbane environment.

Food 8, Service 9, Atmosphere 9

Kech Mara, 3 rue de la Liberté, Gueliz
Tel: 0 24 42 25 32
Open: 7.30am–1 am Mon–Sat. Closed Sundays.   250dh
Moroccan

Run by French brothers Pascal and Arnaud Foltran and Moroccan co-owner Jo Benlolo, Kech Mara has the controversial aim of making a very distinct breach with Moroccan traditions. Not that the place feels subversive in any way. *Au contraire*, it's a bright and breezy – and distinctly retro – place that holds forth a determinedly European aesthetic (retro chairs on the pavement outside, Finnish designer chairs inside, abstract artworks on the walls)

while serving Moroccan food. This fantastically creative yet down-to-earth environment has deservedly become popular with a wide range of people, from young Moroccan students and families to trendies and tourists alike. It's a great hang-out for lunches, casual evening meals or even just for a drink in the evenings, since it has a well-stocked bar. The food isn't overly exhilarating, but it is affordable and tasty. Menus are generally limited to soups and salads and grills, although Friday is couscous day. There's a pleasant terrace upstairs, too, which is a good place to take a drink. At the time of writing the owners were considering live entertainment in the evenings, which would certainly put Kech Mara even further ahead of the pack.

Food 7, Service 8, Atmosphere 8

Kozybar, 47 Place des Ferblantiers, Medina

Tel: 0 24 38 03 24

Open: noon–3pm, 8pm–midnight daily   400dh

International

Despite the booze-specific implications of the name, the Kozybar also operates as a very decent restaurant, tucked away in the corner of the clangorous Place des Ferblantiers. Its dark hallway and elegant downstairs bar area
create an urbane welcome, although you'll be heading upstairs to eat –
either in one of the salons on the middle floor or, if the weather is good
and there is any space left, upstairs on the roof terrace – a fantastic spot
that overlooks the square below and offers views right down to the
Koutoubia. The location makes this a pretty useful lunching spot if you're
schlepping around the Medina. The daytime menu is fairly basic – mostly
sandwiches, soups and salads – although the place somewhat handily

employs the
services of a
Japanese chef
who makes some
kick-ass sushi. At
night, the
Kozybar really
comes into its
own. The square
is quieter, and
dimmed lights
and hip lounge

music create an incredibly seductive environment. The evening menu is
more diverse, offering assorted Moroccan food that includes lamb and fish
tajines, alongside sushi and other meals.

Food 7, Service 8, Atmosphere 8

Ksar Char-Bagh, Palmeraie de Marrakech, Palmeraie.

Tel: 0 24 32 92 44   www.ksarcharbagh.com

Open: noon–2.30pm, 7.30–11pm daily   600dh

International

Until recently, Ksar Char-Bagh's restaurant had a reputation of being one of the finest in the city. Each day young French chef Damien Durand, who studied under Robuchon, Ducasse and Herme, created a superb menu based on fresh market ingredients and produce from extensive orchard and garden that has been created behind the hotel's swimming pool. Durand has

now left and has been replaced by a new chef who has yet to live up to his predecessor's legacy. The tradition of fine food is sure to be maintained, especially when served up in the Ksar's unforgettable high-ceilinged dining room with its vivid black and white colour scheme, but whether it remains one of the must-try places in the city remains to be seen.

Food 8, Service 9, Atmosphere 9

La Maison Arabe, 1 Derb Assehbe, Bab Doukkala, Medina
Tel: 0 24 38 70 10 www.lamaisonarabe.com
Open: noon–2.30pm, 7.30–11pm daily   400dh
Moroccan

Part of the hotel of the same name (see SLEEP), La Maison Arabe's restaurant does not have the stunning visual impact that so many of the Moroccan establishments tend to have. There are no gurgling fountains, *zellijed* walls or strewn rose petals here, but a simple, quiet and somewhat dignified air prevails instead. What is on offer, rare in the Medina, is high-quality à la carte local food – the better 'palace' restaurants tend to have fixed menus with limited choice, which although delicious can be a little restrictive. A range of *tajines* and couscous dishes make up the menu and, while they can be quite conservative in what they offer, they are superbly cooked and full of flavour. As one would expect from this famous name, the service is exemplary and scurrying waiters are always on hand to refill your wine or water glass. After dinner

pop through to the bar, Le Club and enjoy another Marrakech rarity – a well-made cocktail – or a glass of Champagne.

Food 7, Service 8, Atmosphere 8

Le Marrakchi, 52 rue des Banques, Jemaa el Fna, Medina
Tel: 0 24 44 33 77 www.lemarrakchi.com
Open: noon–1am daily   250dh
Moroccan

Le Marrakchi, located opposite the Café de France on the Jemaa el Fna, can be reached by way of dark, incensed stairs that lead up to two separate

floors. The top is the most popular, since it offers superior views across the square – that is, if you arrive there early enough to get one of the few seats close to the main window. The restaurant itself is distinctly Moroccan, and while not as chic as many other spots around, the atmosphere and décor are in harmony with the timeless traditions of the square below. Tables are strewn with rose petals, there's dimmed lighting, and oriental dancers make this a venue suited to group conviviality or quiet intimacy. The menu isn't sophisticated but offers above-average traditional dishes – *pastillas*, *tajines*, couscous – as well as a few pasta and pizza options, and is very reasonably priced. You can dine on fixed-price options or go à la carte. Another bonus: it's the only place on the square where you can get alcohol.

Food 7, Service 8, Atmosphere 7

Narwama, 30 rue de la Koutoubia, Medina
Tel: 0 24 44 08 44
Open: 8pm–12.30am daily   275dh
Thai

Handily located just around the corner from the Koutoubia Mosque off the main square, Narwama is the first restaurant in the medina to offer Thai food. Situated along a scruffy, carpet-lined alleyway (look for the signs near the Hotel Jardins de la Koutoubia) the interior of Narwama is immediately striking. Dark and seductive, the spacious main room is dotted with exotic plants and centred with a dramatic and memorable water-and-fire feature. Pretty waitresses sashay between tables offering outsized menus that offer a range of Thai dishes (classics like Pad Thai, Green Curry and Tom Yam soup) and a range of Moroccan dishes. Though the restaurant boasts two Thai chefs and purports to import ingredients from Asia, the Thai dishes never quite surpass reasonable, and the Moroccan dishes are surprisingly small by Marrakech's normally generous standards (though this may be a blessing for those wishing to bypass the usual feast). In short, the ambience is just as much of a pull as the food, though the latter is perfectly acceptable. If you would like a little more intimacy or some air-con, ask for a seat in one of the smaller salons in the back.

Food 6, Service 7, Atmosphere 8

Salam Bombay, I Avenue Mohammed VI, Hivernage
Tel: 0 24 43 70 83
Open: noon–2.30pm, 7.30–11.30pm daily   300dh
Indian

Marrakchis, notoriously fond of the Bollywood movies that play regularly at Medina cinemas, have never had a restaurant that can offer the glorious tastes, alongside the imported sights, of India. Until now. With huge elephant heads thrusting out of the outside walls, staff decked out in saris and bindis,

and an expansive menu that includes imported Cobra beer and pretty much every Indian dish you'd get in Brick Lane, the Salam does not short-change in terms of creating an authentic experience. Enter through a charming garden, noting the large statue of Shiva on the way in, and take a seat in one of the pink salons or on the outdoor patio (the best spot on a warm evening). The menu is very extensive and very tasty, but even so the chefs are more than happy to rustle up specialities on demand for those more *au fait* with Indian cuisine. Can't be bothered to leave the house? No problem:

the Salam also offers a delivery service, half the price of the normal menu.

Food 8, Service 8, Atmosphere 7

Le Square, corner of the rue de Paris/Avenue Echouhada, Hivernage

Tel: 0 24 42 39 89
Open: 11.30am–3.30pm, 7.30pm–1am Tue–Sun. Closed Mondays.   350dh
Fusion

Formerly known as L'Amandier, this walled garden restaurant is now called Le Square and is run by friendly French couple Guy and Nicky. They have replaced the previously garish colour scheme with something much more sophisticated and easier on the eyes: soft yellows and beiges greet customers as they pass through the garden and into the main dining area, or

make their way to the outside patio, covered by a *mamouni*, to eat al fresco. The menu is Asian–French and dishes are of a very reasonable standard. You can also find traditional Moroccan fare and even sushi (although the latter is not quite as authentic as it could be). If the outdoor tables are taken, the inside isn't a disappointment since the large windows let in lots of light and create a charming, insouciant ambience. It's a quiet, calm place to eat, especially at lunchtimes.

Food 7, Service 7, Atmosphere 8

La Sultana, 403 rue de la Kasbah, Medina

Tel: 0 24 38 80 08 www.lasultanamarrakech.com

Open: 7pm–midnight daily   450dh

Moroccan

La Sultana (see SLEEP), one of the more spectacular hotels in the Medina, boasts over 20 rooms, a wonderful roof terrace, pool, bar, spa – and a restaurant. Dining in hotels you're not staying in is not always such a great experience, but La Sultana is a notable exception, since it offers excellent cuisine in a romantic setting. The setting overall – high-back chairs the size of thrones, large tables, soft music played by a *gnawa* musician the other side

of a gorgeous luminescent pool – may seem on the formal side on arrival, but the stiffness soon fades into a soothing ambience. There are two menus – a Moroccan and an international – both of which feature classic and nouveau dishes; you can choose a fixed three-course meal or mix-and-match starters, mains and desserts according to your taste. The food, cooked by French and Moroccan chefs, is superb and the service is impeccable, although it's a shame the quirky boat-shaped bar won't offer pre- or post-prandial drinks to non-residents. Booking is essential.

Food 8, Service 9, Atmosphere 7

Sur Une Ardoise, Route de Targa, Camp el Ghoul, Guéliz

Tel: 0 24 43 02 29

Open: 12–2.30pm; 7.30–11pm. Closed Sundays & Mondays.   250dh

French

Sur Une Ardoise is a recent addition to Marrakech's ever-expanding gastronomic scene. Situated close to the meeting point of Mohammed V and Mohammed VI on the fringes of Gueliz, it's a short taxi ride to get here but the beaming doorman makes the trip worthwhile – as do the brisk, efficient staff, the low level music and the classic bistro ambience inside (think oblong mirrors, cuboid lamps and huge Jacques Tati film posters). The chef (French, like the owners) likes to infuse his dishes with local Moroccan spices, though the menu – which changes every three months – is resolutely French with lots of adventurous touches (think offal and ingenious fish and meat dishes like carpaccio of shark and rabbit ravioli). An interesting selection of entrees, mains and puddings are on offer at both lunch and dinnertime, though the wine list has quite a lot of catching up to do. The atmosphere can be a little clinical during quiet evenings, but thanks to all the above, that's usually not the case.

Food 8, Service 8, Atmosphere 7

Le Tobsil, 22 Derb Abdellah Ben Hessaien, R'mila Bab Ksour, Medina
Tel: 0 24 44 15 23
Open: 7.30pm–midnight. Closed Tuesdays.   600dh
Moroccan

Tobsil (meaning 'dish' or 'plate' in Arabic) is located deep inside the Bab Laksour area (look out for the signposts for Riad Catalina – Tobsil is next door). It's an elegantly restored *riad* house owned by Christine Rio (whose grandmother was a chef from Brittany) and her photographer husband.

Tobsil is reckoned by many to be the best eating establishment in Marrakech and, while that may be arguable, it certainly resides in the upper echelons of the city's gastronomic scene. The intimate ambience mixes with the exquisite food and excellent service to create a truly memorable experience. Inside the *riad*, tables are placed around the plant-filled

courtyard, in smaller salons and around an upper gallery level. Soft music, sensuous candles and liveried staff create an idyllic atmosphere matched by the glorious food – traditional but refined – that bears down on you as soon as you've settled in, and doesn't stop until way after your belly has started begging for help.

Food 8, Service 9, Atmosphere 9

La Trattoria di Giancarlo, 179 rue Mohammed el Bekal, Gueliz

Tel: 0 24 43 26 41   www.latrattoriamarrakech.com
Open: 7.30–11.30pm. Closed Sunday and lunchtimes.   425dh
Italian

La Trattoria used to be the finest Italian restaurant in town, combining a romantic ambience, crazy décor (courtesy of local American hero Bill Willis), superlative Italian food and exemplary service all in one place. These days a visit can prove to be a somewhat lacklustre experience. The entrance, courtyard and grand salon still bear Willis's surreal signature: stripy chimneys, beguiling ornamentation and quirky detailing. The main dining area is still in the garden, where candles bob mesmerically in a pool, casting a

soft glow over the nearby tables. And waiters dressed in pinstriped suits cater obsequiously to your every whim. The problem is not the ornamentation or the service these days, but the quality of the food. The mix of nouveau and traditional dishes can be decidedly hit-and-miss, and in a setting with so much potential, a miss can only lead to heartbreak.

Food 6, Service 8, Atmosphere 8

drink...

Alcohol is officially frowned on in Muslim culture, but that doesn't seem to stop anyone drinking if they really want to. Morocco's drier than most Western places, of course, but less so than many Islamic countries because of its laid-back attitude to most things.

There isn't exactly a plethora of bars in Marrakech, but there are a few, some of which are well worth visiting. Many bars are annexed to restaurants or hotels since it's easier to get an alcohol licence that way, and these tend to cultivate a somewhat formal atmosphere. There are several independent bars too (mainly in Gueliz) where it's possible to let your hair down a little more, listen to some music and, since many double up as restaurants, perhaps enjoy a meal beforehand.

The Medina, as you might expect given its more traditional cultural status, isn't overrun with places where you can enjoy a cold beer or cocktail, though piano-style hotel bars such as those in the Mamounia and the Hotel Les Jardins de la Koutoubia offer pleasant, if fairly conservative, surroundings. The only really dedicated 'bar' as such is the newly established Kozybar/restaurant, which offers

an urbane bar and an upstairs roof terrace for enjoying pre- or post-dinner (or even lunchtime) drinks. Another option (again recently established) is the new private members' club Kssour Agafay, where you'll find a more formal environment set within a 15th-century *riad*.

Since most of Marrakech's nightlife takes place outside the Medina, it's not surprising that the majority of the city's more trendy watering-holes – such as Le Comptoir, Jad Mahal, Bô-Zin – are located out in Gueliz/Hivernage, or even further out. These venues are restaurants as well, most of them very reputable ones (see Eat), but they are nevertheless good places to hang out and have

drinks since they generate an upbeat atmosphere, especially on weekends when there are often live musicians or DJs, usually favouring a mix of R&B, house, Latino and Oriental/Arabic sounds.

Alcohol is expensive in most places, although more so in nightclubs than bars. In bars, you'll find you have to pay around 30–50dh for a beer or a glass of wine and 50–80dh for a cocktail.

Bô-Zin, Douar Lohna, Route de l'Ourika 3.5km

Tel: 0 24 38 80 12   www.bo-zin.com
Open: 8pm–1am daily

Bô-Zin used to be a little hit-and-miss in the gourmet stakes, and was used as much as a bar/hang-out as an eaterie. These days the food has improved to the extent that it is one of the better places in the city to eat, although the owners have taken great care to ensure it also remains popular with the

party people. The bar here is a good option for drinks, particularly after dinner, and especially in the summer when it's possible to take advantage of the large garden area, with its strategically placed sofas and lounging areas; in winter, you can sit inside on the banquettes enjoying a glass of whisky in front of a roaring fire. The atmospheric interior is great for dancing at weekends when the music gets turned up a notch and the belly-dancers are out in force. The location has its plus and minus points: you'll need a taxi to get here (and although they're quite cheap, this can be a hassle), but it has no neighbours to upset, so the bar can stay open as long and late as the party continues.

Churchill's Piano Bar, Mamounia Hotel, Avenue Bab el Jdid, Medina.

Tel: 0 24 44 44 09   www.mamounia.com
Open: 5pm–1am daily

The Mamounia's refurb will be completed in the late spring of 2007, we expect the Churchill to remain intact and identical. Dress smartly if you want to get in, or the slightly sniffy doormen will turn you away. It's part gentleman's club, part jazz club, and its interior is designed in a classic art-deco-meets-jazz style – soft leather chairs and wall-coverings, a semi-private drinking room off the main bar area, a grand piano in a shallow pit, and runs of bar stools. This is all gently illuminated by backlit painted glass

that features colourful pictures of famous jazz legends and can look spookily ecclesiastical after a couple of the right drinks. You'd be forgiven for thinking the place was kitted out along with the hotel in the 1920s, but in fact it was refitted during the 1980s refurbishment. Still, the ambience seems to work. The bar opens at 5pm each night, plays music (jazz) from 9pm and sells classic whiskies, long drinks, draught and bottled beer and cigars. It's often very quiet but occasionally surprisingly busy, particularly when the film festival is in town.

Le Comptoir, 37 Avenue Echouhada, Hivernage
Tel: 0 24 43 77 02
Open: 5pm–1am Mon–Thurs; noon–1am Fri–Sat

Le Comptoir is more famous as a restaurant than as a bar, but the bar area – located up the sweeping staircase from the main restaurant – is an elegant and entertaining place to go for a drink. In fact, Le Comptoir's glamorous and trendy reputation, sleek design and funky atmosphere make it more appealing than many other more 'dedicated' bars around town, which perhaps explains why it's one of the few places that manages to seem occasionally vibrant even on weekdays. It's decked out in the same manner as the restaurant – curvaceous, stylish, low-lit, comfortable – and you have the benefit of hearing a more considered mix of music here than elsewhere. In keeping with the overall concept of the place, the drinks are fashionably

pricey, but not much more than other hotspots. You can also slink back down the stairwell and out into the garden courtyard if you prefer some horizontal cushion-lounging, although on busy nights you may have to wait a while to get noticed by staff.

Jad Mahal, Fontaine de la Mamounia, Bab Jdid, Hivernage
Tel: 0 24 43 69 84   palaisjadmahal@menara.ma
Open: 7.30pm–1am daily

Part of the Jad Mahal restaurant/club empire in Hivernage, this is one of the few places to catch the local cognoscenti supinely reclining in armchairs and sipping gin and tonics or a cool glass of champagne. Like its neighbour and

competitor Le Comptoir, Jad Mahal provides a sophisticated environment for a relaxing drink, particularly pre- or post-dinner. Entrance is restricted, and unlike many of its large-scale competitors the bar is not full of 'working girls' or elderly tourists clutching guidebooks/maps/camera bags/fanny packs. As the night wears on it begins to fill up with diners wanting an extra drink before they head downstairs to the club. There's also a rooftop terrace overlooking the city walls to one side and out towards the desert on the other, which makes a wonderfully romantic place to sip a cocktail once the sun goes down. More recently the bar area began to introduce live rock/pop acts at weekends.

Kozybar, 47 Place des Ferblantiers, Medina
Tel: 0 24 38 03 24
Open: 12pm–3pm, 8pm–midnight daily

Before the Kozybar appeared in 2005, there really wasn't a funky spot to enjoy a cool beer or refined glass of wine within the walls of the Medina. In

other words, this place – more of a restaurant, despite the name, but with a perfectly decent eponymous bar located near the entrance – is what many regular visitors to the Medina have been waiting for: an intimate place where tourists and Moroccans alike can enjoy fine wines, cognacs and even good cigars from the humidor. Pull up a stool at the bar, snuggle into an intimate booth or lounge up on the attractive terrace, which offers a pleas-antly lounge-style atmosphere with sofas and low tables, and heat lamps in the colder months. The bar itself is very well stocked with assorted wines, spirits and cognacs – they even have cachaça to make authentic caiprinhas.

On certain nights, usually at weekends, you might be lucky enough to witness the unusual combination of an Armenian-born, Moscow-trained piano-player and his bongo-thumping Moroccan sidekick performing a range of jazz and pop standards. On the right night it can turn into an impromptu karaoke session, making this by far the most fun place in the Medina to get wasted.

Kssour Agafay, 52 Sabat Grawa, Kssour
Tel: 0 24 42 70 00   www.kssouragafay.com
Open: 11am–11pm daily

You'd never really notice this Kasbah Agafay (see SLEEP) associated members' club if it wasn't for the funky lanterns that hang incongruously from the ancient roof outside. A beautifully restored 15th-century *riad*, it functions as guesthouse and restaurant as well as a private members' club

open to non-members (a reservation is a must; don't just turn up). The space inside is formal but elegant, and the structure of the *riad* is slightly idiosyncratic in that the main courtyard is on the first floor (there's also a roof terrace). Ascend a narrow stairwell and enter a world of colourful stucco detailing and restored features, enjoy a drink and a cigar in the small bar-fumoir, or browse through one of the cultural books in the library. The venue also organizes regular art exhibitions and parties, although some of these are accessible to paid up members only. You can book for dinner (Moroccan cuisine) here as well, if you fancy making an evening of it.

Le Lounge, 24 rue de Yougoslavie, Gueliz

Tel: 0 24 43 37 03
Open: 10am–1am daily

Le Lounge is a red, vaguely Spanish-themed spot along from the Boule de
Neige and next to the Hotel Diwan that aims to make its customers feel
both stylish and comfortable. There's a small dining space supplemented by
an upper terrace level and an outdoor area, both of which have couch-style

seating and modern artwork on the walls, and double-up as bar hang-outs.
The bar itself is tiny and the TV screens inside the premises don't exactly
promote a rustic charm; but in the summer there are tables outside, making
it one of the few spots where you can enjoy a cool drink in an outside area.
At weekends Le Lounge has DJs that play chilled-out Latino and relaxed
house music to a congruous mix of locals and curious tourists.

Montecristo, 20 rue Ibn Aicha, Gueliz

Tel: 0 24 43 90 31
Open: 8pm–1am daily

The Montecristo used to be one of the better places to go for a drink, but
these days there is a lot of competition and its star is decidedly in the
descendent. The place itself is welcoming enough – a restaurant downstairs
serves up good pasta and pizza dishes; a middle Cuban-themed floor
provides late-night disco action; and an exotic roof terrace functions as a
pre-nightclub bar. Since most people come here towards midnight for the
middle floor, the roof is usually quite empty, making it perfect for a relaxing

drink in the evenings. A very pleasant roof it is too, with low-lit candles and hookah pipes on tables arranged around the perimeter, under the cover of a tent-like canopy and amid decorative foliage. The roof has its own tiny bar that's surprisingly well stocked, offering tasty cocktails, cigars and even pizza (made in the restaurant downstairs). On a warm night it rocks, and if later on you want to imbibe mojitos like they're going out of fashion and get down to the latest R&B/hip hop hits, just wait until after midnight when you're only one floor away from a quite dramatic change of atmosphere.

Nikki Beach, Circuit de la Palmeraie
Tel: 0 24 33 24 94
Open: 11am–finish, daily

Set in the uber-expansive grounds of the Royal Palmeraie Golf Palace, Nikki Beach is the swishest outdoor clubbing mecca Marrakech has thus far seen,

a languorous shrine to elegant slumming and poolside lounging that has been drawing in the crowds since it opened a year or so ago. There's no beach as such – just a series of lounge beds, chilling tents and dining tables arranged around a large pool with its own swim-up bar and serving area. During the daytime a DJ spins lazy soul and laid-back funk while the funky bar staff churn out elaborate cocktails for monied Moroccans and sun-hungry travellers. The cocktail list is good, there's a healthy selection of cold wines and beers, and there are plenty of comfy spots where you can simply kick back and feel great; you can even have a massage (€20). Food here is good quality, so a poolside lunch can be firmly recommended. The only downside is the DJ, who sometimes tries to create a 'party vibe' by pumping the music up to conversation-drowning levels before your lunch is through, and an 'official' 200dh charge to get in (though ask at your *riad* about passes as many of them can arrange free entry).

The Piano Bar, Hotel les Jardins de la Koutoubia, 26 rue de la Koutoubia, Medina
Tel: 0 24 48 88 00
Open: 7pm–midnight daily

The Piano Bar, situated just inside the Jardins de la Koutoubia hotel, is a pleasantly low-key spot for a drink. In contrast to the rest of the fairly

restrained and traditionally decorated ground-floor salon rooms of the hotel, the bar is an assertive combination of reds, blacks, yellow and beiges with a vaguely darkened ambience that borders on louche. There are red stools lined up at the bar, with bow-tied staff attentively awaiting orders, comfortable sofas and a crooner playing the instrument that gave the bar its name (he's even handier on a synthesizer; requests are accepted). There's no dress code to speak of, but the bar overtly aims to attract five-star clientele; it's doubtful you'll be staying long unless you look smart and/or are happy to notch up a decent bill. The bar is rarely busy, making it the perfect place to enjoy a quiet drink and a more private chat.

Le Plage Rouge, Route de l'Ourika, Km 10
Tel: 0 24 37 80 86/0 24 37 80 87
Open: 10am–2am daily

Le Plage Rouge is by far the most ambitious project to hit Marrakech in recent times – which is saying something for a town pretty much defined by its capacity to consistently out-do itself in the charm, audacity and romance stakes. Located 10 kilometres outside the city on the road to Ourika, the 'red beach' is an all-singing, all-dancing hipster complex that loosely follows the concept of Nikki Beach (see page 108) – particularly in the way it calls

itself a beach without offering even a grain of sand. Enter through a court-yard full of boutiques (including a bikini shop and a coiffeur) and into a restaurant decked out in black and reds with an adjacent open-air garden and cocktail bar. If everything goes well, you will get blue skies, chill-out music at reasonable volumes, helpful staff and a fantastic afternoon spent eating, sipping cocktails and dipping in the massive (70 by 30 metres) pool. On a bad day though you may get an incongruous mix of loud hip hop/tuff house, nonchalant staff and overcast skies. Either way, the taxi ride, overpriced food and expensive deckchair/shaded mattress rental (150/400dh) will lighten your wallet considerably.

snack...

Café culture as we know it in the West didn't really exist in Marrakech until recently. There are plenty of cafés around town – some of them even French or European in style – that serve a similar social function to our own, but the difference in terms of comfort, design and overall demographics (in particular the gender balances) is generally acute.

The local preference is for austere, functional places, decorated with obligatory pictures of the King, which serve mint tea, strong espressos, the occasional croissant and, well, not a lot more. Fortunately for latte-lovers and aficionados of the cappuccino, a few places have recently opened that cater more specifically – and knowledgeably – for Western tastes.

We've included a mix of venues, from patisseries such as Amandine, which sell pleasant-tasting sticky things and serve a decent coffee, through souk sanctuaries such as Café des Epices and Café Arabe (both in the Medina), to two of the most Westernized – and most popular – haunts in Marrakech: Grand Café de la Poste and Café du Livre (both in Gueliz).

Dar Cherifa in the Medina is also an interesting place to try out, more a refuge-

cum-gallery than a café, but a great Zen-like space to sip mint tea, survey the art exhibitions, or read one of the history or culture books in the small library there. The fabulous Café du Livre also provides a wonderfully calm escape, with its book-reading, chess-playing clientele and innovative breakfast/lunch menu. For the full hit in terms of European chic and Western-style ambience, try the excellent French bistro Grand Café de la Poste.

Of course, you may want to check out some more local places, in which case the Café du France on the Jemaa el Fna or Les Negoçiants in Gueliz are both institutions in Marrakech. You might also want to sate your sweet tooth with a traditional Moroccan breakfast, which consists of such sugary delights as *sfinge* (doughnuts), *bghrir* (pancake made with yeast) and *msama*, as well as a selection of hot pancakes with butter and honey.

One of the joys of Marrakech is the abundance of fresh oranges. Walking through the Jemaa el Fna can be hard, hot work so stopping to imbibe a glass of refreshing, freshly squeezed OJ at one of the stalls is usually a good idea; alternatively, pick up some dried fruit to munch on the move. In the early evening it might be nice to pop into one of the more anonymous cafés within the Medina and enjoy a glass of mint tea while you unwind with a hookah pipe stuffed with apple tobacco – a true Arabic tradition.

Amandine, 177 rue Mohammed El Bekal, Gueliz
Tel: 0 24 44 96 12
Open: 6am–11pm daily

If it's clean, safe, cake-based fun you're after, look no further than Amandine.
A light, bright patisserie/salon de thé/gelateria, it comprises two sections.
The part to the right of the entrance – polished and shiny – offers tasty

cakes, sweets and ice creams, and has an endearing collection of tiny toy
giraffes behind the counter. You can chew on a peach melba or a *dane
blanche*, or grab a *pain au chocolat* or *toast fromage*. Slightly more relaxed
(especially for smokers) is the café proper next door, which has stools and
seating, more decoration, a spot of music, and a congenial atmosphere. It has
the same range of food and drink options, and there's an upstairs gallery to
complement the main room.

Beldi Country Club, KM 6, Route Du Barrage 'Cherifia'
Tel: 0 24 38 39 50   www.beldicountryclub.com
Open: 10am–8pm daily

The Beldi Country Club is a cross between a botanical wonderland and a
country club retreat. Located about 10 kilometres or so from the Medina, it
requires a little effort to get to, but once you're enveloped in its warm
embrace, you'll probably be glad you did it. Walk through a gorgeous rose
garden to access the main complex, which offers several options: you can
relax in a comfy armchair among splendid Moroccan furnishings and
antiques; make use of the large pool, *hammam* and spa; sip a drink at the

bar; eat *tapas* and enjoy a cocktail at the El Massraf café; or explore the artisan showroom, which sells locally made pottery, ceramics and textiles. With all this on offer in a sophisticated and tranquil environment, it's really worth spending at least an afternoon here, if not a whole day.

Boule de Neige, rue de Yougoslavie, Place Abdelmoumen, Gueliz
Tel: 0 24 44 60 44
Open: 5am–11pm daily

Next to the Hilton's eye-wateringly delicious patisserie, Boule de Neige offers a dark green and pink interior and a pleasant sunny patio with wicker chairs shaded by umbrellas. The only real food – apart from the sticky bun collection near the counter – is breakfast (continental 30dh, American

50dh), served between 8 and 11am, although the patio is a good spot to grab a drink anytime. The staff couldn't care less if you have a nice day but despite the sullen service they don't mind if you pop next door and bring back a pastry or two. There is an upstairs salon, which is about as inviting as the frumpy downstairs section.

Café Arabe, 184 rue El Mouassine, Medina
Tel: 0 24 42 97 28 www.cafearabe.com
Open: 10am–midnight daily

Until Café Arabe came on the scene, there were no Western-style cafés in the heart of the Medina; or at least nowhere that offered a decent lunch and a glass of rosé. Unlike the charming but limited Café des Epices, Arabe offers a full range of meals centred mainly around a Moroccan and Italian menu that's all pastas, soups and salads, plus a good selection of drinks and wines. It's a wonderfully pleasant place to be. The entrance leads from a dusty street into a frondescent open-air courtyard with walls of Marjorelle

blue and a close-knit community of tables. There's an interior salon at the back with more tables and also a roof terrace that opens only in the summer. Café Arabe is an incredibly popular place, not only because it's one of the few refined sanctuaries within the souk, but because the food is good, the prices are reasonable and the service benign. All-round, an attractive lunch (or even dinner) venue for anyone needing a break from the hustle-bustle of the pink maze.

Café des Epices, 75 Rahba Lakdima, Medina

Tel: 0 24 39 17 70   www.cafedesepices.com
Open: 9am–close daily

Set snugly into a corner of the old spice market where old women gather to sell knitted woolly hats and older men sit and sell spices, the Café des Epices is the perfect spot for taking a break from the heat and hassle of the

souks. The building has three floors, including a refreshing roof terrace that affords good views across the Medina, and is basic but charming, with terracotta and white walls, small chalked menus on wooden tables and a narrow stairwell that runs up the side. The menu is correspondingly simple – fresh juices, teas and coffees, a smattering of sandwiches, the occasional omelette, salads – but the staff (mostly young, internationally minded men, very healthy since they have to run up and down the narrow stairs all day) emit a down-to-earth, genuine friendliness; and with sandwiches going for 30dh, salads for 40dh and simple breakfasts available from 9am this is a definite boon for the Medina. Grab a table downstairs or near a window on the second floor if you want to watch the ever-colourful comings and goings of the spice market.

Café de France, Jemaa el Fna, Medina

Open: 6am–11pm daily

Café de France doesn't go big on decorative chic, but nonetheless it's one of the best-known places on the Jemaa el Fna. Its large dimensions and excellent location make it a convenient meeting-point, and ensure that it's always busy with a healthy mix of locals and tourists. There is a lunch and dinner menu, but the food isn't particularly inspiring and the service is usually whimsical at best (we recommend you take the short walk to such restaurants as Terraces d'Alhambra, Le Marrakchi or even Chez Chegrouni next door). What

does make it worthwhile, however, is the open terraces where you can go for a drink and a convivial chat. The top floor especially affords great views over the square. If you're lucky they'll be making fresh crêpes in the morning (no one seems to know when they will do this). Don't worry if the veteran staff ignore you for a while either – they do that to everyone and it has now become part of the place's charm.

Café du Livre, 44 rue Tarik Ben Ziad, Gueliz
Tel: 0 24 43 21 49 www.cafedulivre.com
Open 9.30am–9pm. Closed Mondays.

Run by the amiable, people-loving Sandra Zwollo, this brand new bookshop,

café and restaurant opened in January 2006 and has already become a prime hang-out for everyone from local literati types to studious Moroccans in search of a quiet place to read. Located just down the road from the well-known Catanzaro restaurant, the place is slightly hidden away through an archway and within the grounds of a somewhat scruffy hotel. To walk through the glass door, however, is to enter a Zen-like world of relaxed music, muffled chat and slick chess moves. To the left is a well-stocked book-shop/reading area; to the right, a more conventional café with dining tables, the lightest 19th-century Persian decorative touches and a fireplace that crackles alive in winter. The menu focuses on simple, home-made, fresh dishes like risottos and succulent speared kebabs, all for very reasonable prices. There are decent breakfast options too: the weekend brunch is very popular, as is the WiFi the café recently had installed. A recent alcohol licence has made the place popular in the evenings as well as the daytime.

Café les Negoçiants, 110 Angle Avenue Mohammed V et Boulevard Zerktouni, Gueliz
Tel: 0 24 43 57 82
Open: 6am–11pm daily

A curious question raised by Café les Negoçiants, an attractive and cosmo-politan café in the centre of Gueliz, is this: why would you bother spearing a toastie with a cocktail stick when all there is to keep inside is a slice of

processed cheese? Such burning issues are unlikely ever to be addressed, but it doesn't really matter because the reason to come here is not the food (although the breakfasts are decent); the strength of Negoçiants is its terrific ambience. In fact, it's massively popular with the locals, many of whom recline on the rattan seating out front, watching the action on the perpetually busy Abdel Moumen from beneath the distinctive green-and-white awning. The clientele is mixed, too, especially for Moroccan cafés, which are usually male-dominated. Business folk, gay crowds, families and hipsters all warm to Negoçiants' broad appeal.

Dar Cherifa/Café Literaire, 8 Derb Charfa Lakhir Mouassine, Medina

Tel: 0 24 42 64 63   www.marrakech-riads.net
Open: 9am–7pm daily

An oasis of calm in a crazy city full of odours and noise, Dar Cherifa has to be experienced at least once during a trip to the Medina. It is one of the most majestic *riads* in town, founded by Abdelatif Ben Abdellah (of Marrakech Riads fame – their offices are upstairs), who has transformed the place into an art gallery, library and general shrine to inner peace. Visiting the place, with its elegant columns, relaxation salons and  tranqil, contemplative atmosphere, is like receiving an architectural massage. Exhibitions change every few weeks and vary in theme (and quality), but there is a permanent photography exhibit (upstairs) that documents the sensitive restoration of the space three years ago. There's also a small but perfectly formed library of books on Moroccan and French culture, and you can take a mint tea or coffee here for 20dh.

Grand Café de la Poste, 127 Avenue Mohammed V, Gueliz

Tel: 0 24 43 30 38
Open: 9am–1am daily

By far the trendiest place to lunch in Marrakech, the Grand Café De La Poste – located directly across from the main post office on Mohammed V – is a direct emulation of a classic 1920s French bistro, complete with rattan chairs, charming outdoor terrace and an elegant, spacious interior. The outside terrace is the most popular place to hang out; separated from the busy Mohammed V by a fence that allows striated glimpses of the world outside, the Grand Café is where many of the city's

'dahlings' converge to take advantage of the sophisticated menu, impeccable service and congenial atmosphere. Inside the café are more tables and a grand staircase leading up to an informal Moroccan-style deck that's kitted out with comfy sofas, soft cushions and low tables. The café's menu is one of the best in town, offering great breakfast and lunch options, as well as refined evening meals. The place favours French-style dishes but stretches to other European and Moroccan dishes as well. Of course you have to pay for this; the hottest place to lunch in town is, as you might expect, also the most expensive.

Nid' Cigogne, 60 Place des Tombeaux Saadiennes, Kasbah, Medina

Tel: 0 24 38 20 92
Open: 9am–11pm daily

An unprepossessing place (to say the least) from the outside, Nid' Cigogne is nonetheless a bit of a godsend, offering shaded respite and a good menu when the going gets hot down in the Kasbah. It's handily located opposite the Saadian tombs, the walls of which the local storks like to use as a meeting-place and lavatory, and is, interestingly enough for a Moroccan café, run entirely by women. After the initial ascent up the shabby staircase, you

reach a covered terrace that looks directly down on the entrance to the tombs and the usually busy square around it. Behind is another, prettier roof terrace which uses plants and vines to good effect, and a mezzanine level with a couple of wicker chairs set up for an intimate chinwag. The menu is surprisingly extensive and inexpensive – portions are large – and is very good to vegetarians. Choose from such dishes as couscous, salads, *tajines*, omelettes, and hot and cold soups. Those with a sweet tooth and a keen eye for cakes will have probably already spotted the convenient neighbouring patisserie on the way in.

Nikki Beach, Palmeraie Golf Palace, Palmeraie
Tel: 0 24 30 10 10 www.nikkibeach.com
Open: 9.30am–5pm, 6pm–midnight daily

With its shimmering pool, sexy ambience, classy chill-out music, extravagant

sun-loungers and competent menu, Nikki Beach is a great option for those looking to lunch in a somewhat hip environment – especially those who might fancy a post-prandial paddle. It costs to get out here, of course, but the benefit is that once you've finished your lunch you can spend the day sipping cocktails, enjoying the sounds and splashing around in the water. The menu offers a good range of international dishes, from stir-fries and salads to pasta and a great selection of fish and seafood. Dining by the pool is naturally a pleasant experience on a nice day, and although the staff are not always so attentive the service is generally quite good. The prices are slightly higher than average, so making a day of it definitely makes sense. If you're feeling stressed you can even buy a back-rub from one of the resident masseuses. The only downside might be the DJ, who sometimes tries to create a 'party vibe' by pumping the music up to conversation-drowning levels before your lunch is through.

Patisserie de Princes, 32 rue Bab Agnaou, Medina
Tel: 0 24 40 30 33
Open: 5am–11pm daily

Patisserie de Princes is possibly the most famous sweet shop in Marrakech, located on the budget-traveller strip known as the rue Bab Agnaou, leading just off the Jemaa el Fna. It's the place to head if you are enamoured with all things sugary and powdery and/or partial to the occasional delicious milkshake. It's also very convenient if you simply want to dive out of the heat and into somewhere coolly air-conditioned. The front of the shop is full of cakes and pastries, all temptingly laid out in chilled glass cabinets. Once you've bought your treats you can pass through to the popular back room or up to the grand salon, and mingle with the locals and tourists while, predictably, pictures of the King stare down at you from the walls.

party...

Marrakech's nightspots are a direct extension of the local bar scene. In other words, there are predominantly 'hotel' nightclubs that range from the uninspiring to the quite alarming, with only one independent venue – Pacha – offering anything like a 'real' clubbing experience.

The best of the rest are listed below. They have been selected because they offer a good mix of tourists and locals, together with a more contemporary (if not overly diverse) spread of music, and – although dedicated clubbers may look down their noses – they can be a lot of fun on the right night if you leave your preconceptions at the door.

As with the bars, most of the nightclubs are located in Gueliz, although New Feeling and Pacha are further out of town. There is another similarity with the bar scene: a barely concealed sex industry exists, so men should be aware that girls who show an interest will usually have money rather than romance on their mind.

Many of the nightclubs share a similar music policy, which is suspiciously similar to that of the bars, and the interiors are laid out in much the same way – a large, main dance-floor surrounded by tables and booths, often overlooked by a circular terrace where you can have a drink and watch events unfold from a distance.

The price of drinks in the clubs is high by European standards: 50–90dh for a beer and 90–110dh for a cocktail is quite normal. If you are with a few people it might make sense to purchase a bottle from the bar in advance and keep it on the table; this usually gets the admission charge (usually between 100–150dh, often including a drink) waived and so can work out cheaper.

There are upsettingly few places to experience live music in Marrakech. Venues such as VIP and other small, local venues occasionally put on traditional oriental cabaret, which can involve mini-orchestras and singers and dancers covering popular and classical songs from the Arab world. More often than not, these shows involve a man in exceedingly tight trousers warbling dramatically over a selection of synthesized Casio beats. It's an acquired taste.

For the more fiscally adventurous, the casinos also offer alternative late-night entertainment. The best and more interesting ones are at the Mamounia and Es Saadi hotels. The Mamounia is far more glamorous inside, while the Es Saadi has a spectacular exterior with flames leaping from the centre of the fountain. One can bet with relatively small stakes, so don't feel too over-awed by the pseudo-glitz.

Diamant Noir, Hotel Marrakech, Place de la Liberté, Avenue Mohammed V, Gueliz

Tel: 0 24 43 43 51
Open: 11pm–4am daily

Every place has its institutional nightspot; Marrakech has the Black Diamond. It's not a dive exactly, but it doesn't meet the often ice-cool standards (décor wise) of the other bars. Rather, it's a no-frills nightclub of the kind found across the globe, attracting a mix of young students and an upbeat gay crowd who between them drum up a vibrant atmosphere, especially at weekends. Feel the jaded aura of the place as you walk through the less-than-glamorous entrance and mooch into the two-tiered discothèque proper. The top-floor bar (where 'ladies' often gather to preen and perch on stools) has some comfortable seating, a DJ booth and a couple of pool tables in case it's a quiet night. Downstairs is dominated by a mirrored dance-floor, more seating and another couple of bars. Don't be

too quick to judge, though: on the right night it can be surprisingly good, down-to-earth fun.

Jad Mahal, Fontaine de la Mamounia, Bab Jdid, Hivernage

Tel: 0 24 43 69 84 palaisjadmahal@menara.ma
Open: midnight–5am Thurs–Sat

The third part of the Jad Mahal empire (see EAT & DRINK) is its über-chic club, the pet project of Jean Jacques Garella (one of the three fashionistas who own the place). He enjoys an elevated position in the French fashion hierarchy, and the interior shows more than a passing interest in the work of Versace. Purple and leopard-skin abound, with specially designed double stools/sofas behind the bar a unique feature. Determined to keep the

'working girls' at bay, they claim to let in only one in five who approach the velvet ropes. The clientele are the wealthy and glamorous, who come to dance the night away free from sleaze and intrusion. Currently an in-house DJ works the decks playing a mixture of house and club classics, but there are moves afoot to introduce some more well-known international names. At present the club has plans to expand to every day of the week.

Montecristo, 20 rue Ibn Aicha, Gueliz
Tel: 0 24 43 90 31
Open: 11pm–1.30am

The roof terrace might be relaxed and intimate (see DRINK) but come midnight the middle floor of Montecristo comes alive and Marrakech's nightlife begins in earnest. Broadly speaking, this is the place to be for a large percentage of the city's youth. It's the floor where the Cuban theme is most pronounced, too – not just not cigars on sale, but Che Guevara posters behind the bars, barmen sporting panamas, tasty mojitos and the occasional member of staff bursting into spontaneous bursts of salsa dancing. Of course it's a very thin veneer, but Montecristo is nonetheless busy enough most nights to create a decent atmosphere. There's not a great deal of seating, so get settled early if you don't want to be left standing. The upstairs remains open in case an escape route is required.

New Feeling, Palmeraie Golf Palace, Palmeraie
Tel: 0 24 30 10 10
Open: 11pm–3.30am daily

Perhaps it's the fact the crowds have some excess cash, or maybe it's just the buzz of a hot new nightspot, but the fact that New Feeling is way out in the Palmeraie doesn't seem to deter anyone from going. It costs 100dh each way, but since it has the reputation for being the best place in town and attracts a lot of the city's cognoscenti, it's largely worth it (taxi drivers, without fail, recommend it as the place to be – but they would, wouldn't they?). The venue attempts to pitch itself at an upmarket crowd, and is in the same league as Jad Mahal and Theatro (with whom it competes for the

title of Marrakech's best venue). Tell-tale signs are the Lichtenstein and Haring prints on the walls, and the plethora of shirts and trousers as opposed to jeans and sneakers. The main dance-floor has a ritzy glass podium for the

principal movers and shakers, and space enough for anyone else who wants to join in. The crushed-glass bar is a nice touch, although the prices aren't quite so cool. The obligatory curved seats encircle the dance-floor and an upper gallery that's normally fairly empty. If you are staying in the Palmeraie at one of the sophisticated villa/palace/kasbah hotels, then this is your best option for a late night drink.

Pacha, Boulevard Mohamed VI, Zone Hotelière de l'Aguedal

Tel: 0 24 38 84 00   www.pachamarrakech.com
Open: noon–5am daily

Despite the huge increase in worldwide tourism to Marrakech over the last decade or so, the city has always lacked a nightspot with decent connections to the global club scene. Not any more. Pacha, one of the world's leading club brands, was always an obvious candidate to bring some international clubbing savvy to the city, and they finally took a chance and flung open their doors to the Marrakchi cognoscenti in 2005. It's more a complex than a club, with a spacious chill-out lounge, two restaurants and a pool, although the club takes prominence. Capable of housing 1,500 people, it's

the largest club venue – and the largest sound system – in Africa. For anyone seriously into clubbing this is really the only spot to head for on Friday and Saturday nights. It's a bit of a trek out of town, but here, and only here, will you find the likes of Pete Tong, Sasha, Tiesto and Eric Morillo, all of whom have played here alongside locals such as DJ Scream and Kosta Kritikos. You can make a night of it by eating in the very good Crystal restaurant (see EAT) beforehand or just hanging out in the chill-out lounge. The crowds, predominantly young and Moroccan, always seem up for a good time, and although week nights can be good, Saturday is 'international guest' night.

Paradise, Kempinski Mansour Eddahbi, Avenue de France, Hivernage
Tel: 0 24 33 91 00
Open: 10.30pm–4am daily

Paradise is one of the flashier clubbing locales in town, popular with wealthy locals and ex-pats alike. It's bigger than most of the other clubs, with a 1,500

capacity, and is characterized by a clutter of chintzy lights and ostentatious decoration. There's a staircase that sweeps heroically downstairs to the main bar area, a large dance-floor overlooked by a state-of-the-art DJ box, lots of intimate and comfortable seating and table arrangements (which fill up as the night wears on: they can be reserved in advance), and an upper terrace that features a massive video screen on one side and a perpetually deserted salad bar on the other. Power-dressed men cavort with under-dressed 'ladies' to the familiar sounds of R&B, hip-hop and Arabic music, and occasionally the place gets carried away with itself and a less self-conscious atmosphere emerges.

Theatro, Hotel Es Saadi, Avenue el Quadissia, Hivernage

Tel: 0 24 44 88 11
Open: 10pm–4am daily

The man who started the Es Saadi hotel – Frenchman Jean Bauchet – once managed the famed Moulin Rouge in Paris. After building a casino then a hotel here, he also built a theatre and put on not just plays but also musicians such as Dizzy Gillespie. The theatre closed down a few years ago,

but was reopened at the end of 2002 in its new guise as nightclub, overseen by Bauchet's grandson Jean-Alexandre. The place has had an upmarket refurbishment, giving the interior a much more modern look (with designer furniture, strategically placed tables and a large and very expensive bar) while retaining its original structure. At weekends Theatro offers some seriously good times, with live drummers, sexy dancers on the stage and some pretty good house music. It can also become seriously packed. You can book a table in advance, which comes with a bottle of spirits – at a substantial cost of course. Housed beside the casino, the plethora of top-of-the-range sports cars parked outside testifies to the kind of monied, 'up-for-it' clientele who frequent Theatro.

Totem, Hotel Royal Mirage Deluxe, rue de Paris, Hivernage

Tel: 0 63 79 17 86/0 61 24 24 63
Open: 11pm–5am

Totem is one of the more recent hotspots in Marrakech, having opened its doors in January 2006. A relatively small space, it boasts a reasonably sized dance-floor, a snazzy bar and rows of white(ish) tables and chairs arranged around the main floor. In other words, it's much like most of the other hotel

clubs in town. Totem has a slight edge over others, however, in that DJ Costa (not to be confused with the Kosta that plays at Pacha) has residencies in Spain and Paris and seems to know his stuff. The crowds aren't clued-up clubbers, exactly – more a mix of businessmen, local girls and curious tourists – but Costa keeps them entertained with a knowing mix of disco, deep house, R&B and Latino music.

VIP, Place de la Liberté, Avenue Mohammed V, Gueliz
Tel: 0 24 43 45 69
Open: 10pm–4am daily

This place used to be known as 'Star's House'. Then they ripped the inside out, refurbished it and renamed it, and now it's called VIP. Seemingly it has done the place wonders, since it's gone from being regarded as a mediocre

venue into a pretty decent place for a night out. Any nervousness provoked by the neon tunnel that leads downstairs should be disregarded. As soon as you take a right turn into the venue proper you find what is perhaps the closest the city centre gets to a normal nightclub – more neon, a swish bar and lots of seating. The DJ seems to know his house and techno a bit better than many others, and is quite capable of whipping the floor into a frenzy. Turn left after the aforementioned tunnel and you end up in the midst of quite a different scene – the surreal world of Moroccan cabaret where musicians passionately saw strings and hammer synths, and singers and dancers entertain a mostly local crowd. You can skip happily from room to room, but the management somewhat meanly prevents you taking your drinks in between.

CASINOS

Es Saadi, Avenue el Qadissia, Hivernage
Tel: 0 44 44 88 11 www.casinodemarrakech.com
Open: 4pm–4am daily

The Es Saadi casino, situated 50 metres from the hotel, has an old-fashioned air in keeping with the nostalgic feel of the hotel itself. The hotel remains a family-run business, and grandmother can still be found counting up at the

end of the night. The facilities inside the vast space are up-to-date, with video slot machines next to more traditional games such as craps, stud poker, punto blanco, blackjack and roulette. On Fridays you can enjoy a traditional meal with a Moroccan 'spectacular' beforehand.

La Mamounia Casino, Mamounia Hotel, Avenue Bab Jdid, Medina

Tel: 0 44 38 86 44/43 www.mamounia.com

Open: 4pm–5am daily

La Mamounia's vast, vaulted casino has a slightly faded opulence that some might consider charming. The cavernous interior is more reminiscent of Vegas than it is of Marrakech. It has obviously seen many fortunes won and lost, and has played host to some worthy gamblers. Here the well-heeled Marrakchi mix with the international jet-set to create an expensive and rarefied atmosphere. There is a separate restaurant and bar area, and the main hall is set up for roulette, blackjack, poker and

baccarat, and is also equipped with more than a hundred gaming machines. Be warned, you will not be allowed in if you are untidy – and that, I'm afraid, means no blue jeans or trainers.

Notes & Updates

culture...

Marrakech isn't one of those holiday destinations that's brimming with monuments and museums. The city's principal allure stems not from sightseeing, but from the everyday magic that pervades the streets – the exotic sights and sounds that seem so mysterious and compelling to Western senses.

The best way to sample the city is to wander the labyrinthine streets of the Medina, where a surprise awaits around every corner, and where you can spend hours simply absorbing the bewitching hustle-bustle that has its roots in traditions a thousand years old.

That said, Marrakech does have its own cultural heritage – the Koutoubia Mosque; the Saadian Tombs; the Ben Youssef Medersa (Koranic school); the awe-inspiring craftsmanship on view inside the Marrakech Museum; and of course the dilapidated ruins of the Badii Palace. A visit to the anthropologically appointed Dar Tiskiwin is also rewarding, and for a pleasurable stroll, there are the city's many gardens.

Each of these will help you build a picture of a fascinating city, although anticipate some frustrations: the Koutoubia is only open to Muslims; the Agdal Gardens seem to open quite randomly (weekends are your best bet, except for those when the King is in residence); and you'll need quite a powerful imagination to fill in the large gaps at the Badii.

Most of the gardens, however, are a joy, a real oasis away from the chaos. The Majorelle Gardens, owned by Yves Saint Laurent, offer a delightful refuge from busy Gueliz (and also incorporate an interesting museum), while the Mamounia's gardens down in the Medina are similarly enchanting.

Turning to contemporary culture, Marrakech seems to be full of ex-pat designers, photographers, painters, sculptors and film-makers, whereas the activities of the local arts community appear to be less vibrant – or at least largely well hidden. That said, although literature and the visual arts tend to be dominated by past masters, a younger, more contemporary scene is now start-ing to emerge: check out the Matisse and Bleue galleries for examples of fresh Moroccan painters, and the annual Marrakech Film Festival for works by both international and local film-makers.

The film festival, inaugurated in 1999, is a cause of celebration for the town and the largely international coverage that has followed has helped give the city a more artistic and cosmopolitan image.

Badii Palace, Place de Ferblantiers, Mellah, Medina
Open: 8.30–11.45am, 2.30–5.45pm daily
Admission: 10dh

What was once part of a sumptuous palace, built by Ahmed El Mansour in the 16th and 17th centuries, is now just a smattering of battered ruins. So opulent was the palace that it reportedly took 25 years to complete. A hundred years later, however, it was raided and all the treasure sent elsewhere. Nowadays, it's pretty stark. There isn't even a gate, just a hole in one of the palace walls, which leads into a vast area dominated by sunken spaces that

once housed flourishing gardens and a grand reflecting pool. The ruins still contain a few trees and there are also some excavated remains of caves and passages and some well-weathered original floor mosaics. Apart from that it's just you, your imagination, and the storks that use the battlements as latrines.

Bahia Palace, Riad Zitoun el Jdid, Medina
Tel: 0 24 38 92 21
Open: 8.30–11.45am, 2.30–5.45pm daily
Admission: 10dh

The Bahia Palace was originally constructed by the infamous vizier Ba Ahmed Ben Moussa in the early 1900s. When he died it was inhabited by the French *resident-generaux* and is today used for a range of purposes – King Mohamed VI famously threw a party here for US rap star P. Diddy (formerly Puff Daddy) in 2002. The palace is undeniably elegant, incorporating grand columns, stunning stucco and runs of *zellije* throughout the main

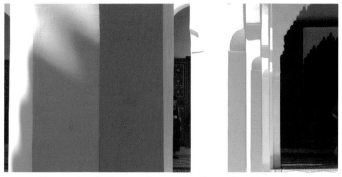

areas, with countless bedrooms that used to house Ben Moussa's numerous 'other halves' (four wives and 24 concubines, to be exact).

Ben Youssef Medersa, Place Ben Youssef, Medina
Tel: 0 24 39 09 11/2
Open: 9am–6pm
Admission: 20dh

A *medersa* is a Koranic school, specifically built for the teaching of Islamic law and scripture. This particular one was built in the 14th century and enlarged to its present size in 1564. It's in remarkable shape, primarily because it was still in use up until the 1960s, and is a stunning place to visit.

A long corridor leads into a large, tranquil central space with a pool. At one end of the room is a prayer closet in which lecturers delivered their lessons, backs to their audience to make use of the dome's natural acoustics. Around the central courtyard are scores of ascetic, cell-like rooms, which were used as student quarters.

Jemaa el Fna
Medina

All roads lead to the Jemaa el Fna, so you're bound to wind up here at some point. Although it's dubbed 'the square' (or '*la place*') it's actually more of an irregular 'L' shape and is as old as the city itself. A vivacious display of local life and colour night and day, it's largely untouched by Western influences and maintains traditions that stretch back over a millennium. Daytime in the square is relatively restrained by night-time's upbeat standards, but there's always something happening: snake-charmers, scribes, tattooists, musicians and beggars sit or hobble between alluring stalls offering everything from freshly squeezed orange juice to great mounds of dried fruit. Come sunset, the music grows louder and '*la place*' comes to life as storytellers, potion-sellers, magicians, acrobats, dentists, transvestite dancers and

other assorted figures join the festivities. Oh, and a thousand and one food stalls are set up to create one of the most photogenic barbecues in the world.

Koutoubia Mosque
Jemaa el Fna, Medina

Paris has the Eiffel Tower, London has Big Ben – and Marrakech has the Koutoubia Mosque. Towering over the square (and over the whole of the Medina), it's the highest point in the city by a long way and the landmark with which visitors become most acquainted. 'Koutoubia' means 'of the

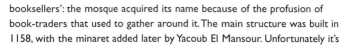

booksellers': the mosque acquired its name because of the profusion of book-traders that used to gather around it. The main structure was built in 1158, with the minaret added later by Yacoub El Mansour. Unfortunately it's

only the outside you'll be seeing unless you're a Muslim, and that from a slight distance, since non-Muslims are barred from the interior and most of the surrounding area.

Saadian Tombs, rue de Kasbah, Bab Agnaou, Medina
Open: 8.30–11.45am, 2.30–5.45pm daily
Admission: 10dh

The Saadian Tombs are located right next to the Badii Palace. They're small in size but huge in cultural significance, since they contain the sacred mausoleums of the grand sultans of the Saadian era. They were discovered by

accident in the 1920s by the French military, a fantastic find since the low, mosaic tombs inside actually pre-date the Saadian era. The main attractions are three pavilions, which include a Prayer Hall and the Hall of Twelve Columns, containing the tombs of various Alaouite princes plus the Saadian sultan Ahmed El Mansour, his son and grandson.

GALLERIES AND MUSEUMS

Dar Tiskiwin, 8 rue de la Bahia, Medina
Tel: 0 24 38 91 92
Open: 9.30–12.30pm, 3.30–5.30pm daily
Admission: 15dh

Dar Tiskiwin is the concept of Dutch anthropologist Bert Flint. A keen collector of Berber antiquities from rugs and tables to jewellery and clothing, he decided a few years ago to open up his private treasures to the public. They are housed in a typically labyrinthine *riad,* which still functions as his home. A permanent exhibition includes an imaginary 'trail' along the old nomadic cara-

van routes and offers information on – as well as cultural artefacts from – sub-Saharan tribes that are not much mentioned in writings or oral traditions, with the aim of preserving the cultures of these communities.

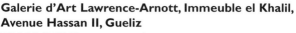

Galerie d'Art Lawrence-Arnott, Immeuble el Khalil, Avenue Hassan II, Gueliz

Tel: 0 24 43 04 99 www.arnott-lawrence.com
Open: 10am–12.30pm, 4–7pm Mon–Fri; 10am–12.30pm Sat

Philip Arnott and John Lawrence first became business partners in London in 1975. Having been associated with major galleries in London and Tangiers

(as well as currently acting as North African representatives for the British auction house, Bonham's), the pair now bring their long history of art appreciation to Marrakech. Focusing on a wide range of Moroccan art, from painting to embroidery, both traditional and contemporary, Lawrence-Arnott has succeeded in bringing some much-needed diversity to the city's gallery scene.

Musée d'Art Islamique, Majorelle Gardens, Avenue Yacoub El Mansour, Gueliz

Open: daily, 8am–noon, 3–7pm in summer; 8am–noon, 2–5pm in winter
Admission: 15dh. No children. Dogs and picnics forbidden.

The inviting, boldly blue building in the Majorelle Gardens is the Museum of Islamic Art. It used to be the studio of Jacques Majorelle (who gave the gardens as well as the blue colour his name), but was renovated into a neat little space displaying all kinds of artefacts and decorations relating to Islamic art.

143

Through several small rooms, a range of Irke pottery, polychrome plates,
jewellery, antique doors and other assorted exhibits are displayed.

Musée de Marrakech, Place Ben Youssef, Medina
Tel: 0 24 39 09 11/2
Open: 9.30am–6pm daily
Admission: 30dh

Back in 1997 the government renovated this grandiose 20th-century house
into an impressive gallery space, and thus it's a dual attraction. There's the
building itself, which consists of a network of different-sized rooms that
have been converted into show spaces, yet whose design – such as the

immense UFO-style chandelier in the main hall – and decoration are
absorbing. Then there are the exhibitions, all temporary, which focus on
'heritage' art in the central hall, and contemporary art in the *douiria* (a guest
apartment) and *hammam*. There is also a neat little café just near the door,
which comes in very handy in hot weather.

GARDENS

Agdal Gardens, Royal Palace, Medina
Open: sporadically, but usually at weekends. Closed when the King is in
residence.

These gardens were built in the 12th century during the Almohad dynasty. Located at the back of the Royal Palace, they comprise vast (40-acre) gardens and orchards that incorporate pomegranates, figs, oranges, walnuts and

vineyards. There are some pavilions scattered around but the showpiece of the gardens is a huge pool right in the centre, which was once used for swimming practice by the sultan's soldiers and claimed the life of at least one sultan.

Majorelle Gardens, Avenue Yacoub El Mansour, Gueliz

Open: daily, 8am–noon, 3–7pm in summer; 8am–noon, 2–5pm in winter
Tel: 0 24 30 18 52   www.jardinmajorelle.com
Admission 20dh. No children. Dogs and picnics forbidden.

The Majorelle Gardens, today owned by Yves Saint Laurent, were primarily

the project of French artist Jacques Majorelle (son of celebrated furniture maker Louis Majorelle), who opened them to the public in 1947. The collection of plants was started in the 1920s, imported from five continents in order to create an overwhelming jumble of floral exotica. Palms, cacti and bamboo all thrive in this small but enchanting place, amid attractive walkways, a lilied pool, and the Museum of Islamic Art (see page 143). Walking through the gardens is akin to a visit to the Eden Project, with every different plant annotated for the visitor's information, and the keen gardener can spend hours sitting in the shade admiring the prime examples of the different species.

Mamounia Gardens, Mamounia Hotel, Avenue Bab Jdid, Medina

Tel: 0 24 38 86 00 www.mamounia.com

The Mamounia Hotel (see SLEEP) actually takes its name from its gardens, which are over a hundred years older, laid out by Prince Moulay Mamoun in the 18th century. The gardens aren't huge but the orange and olive trees, colourful flowerbeds and assorted flora are all meticulously maintained and together create a charming environment. If you fancy a stroll round the gardens it's best to dress smartly, and it might also be worth combining your visit with a buffet lunch or afternoon tea to guarantee admission.

Menara Gardens, Avenue de la Menara, Hivernage

Open: 5am–6.30pm daily
Admission: free. Picnic pavilion 15dh.

The Menara Gardens consist of a large basin of water surrounded by fertile orchards. The water basin goes back to the 12th-century Almohad era, although the green pavilion (which affords great views of the basin from the first floor) was added in the 19th century. You can spot the carp swimming

in the water, stroll in the orchards or picnic in the pavilion. Come night-time, the place hosts a fantasia – with 'spectacular' 3D colour re-enactments of famous historical battles.

shop...

The principal shopping attraction in Marrakech are the souks. A honeycomb of intricately connected alleyways, this fundamental section of the old city is a micro-medina in itself, comprising a dizzying number of stalls and shops that range from itsy kiosks no bigger than an elf's wardrobe to scruffy store-fronts that morph into glittering Aladdin's caves once you're inside.

Strolling through the souks is a must, even if you're only intending to sample the unique atmosphere – but if that is your intention, just make sure you don't make too much eye contact or you'll soon be cajoled into parting with your hard-earned cash.

Traditionally, the souks were divided into different areas – one for metalwork, one for leather, one for carpets, and so on. These areas can still be vaguely discerned, although there has been a certain degree of cross-pollination over the last few years. You can purchase brightly coloured *baboush* (those pointy Arabian Nights style slippers the locals sport), carpets, kaftans and *djellabahs* (traditional Muslim attire for men and women), lanterns, rugs, leather bags and yes, even camels, from many different sections of the markets.

If the upside is that there are so many exotic-looking things on offer, the downside is that much of it is the same. The compact structure of the markets and speedy skills of its resident artisans means that anything that sells well is quickly replicated. And replicated. And replicated…

Prolonged retail exploration within this environment is an art form. With the right mindset it's a lot of fun; with the wrong one, a disaster. There's plenty to 'ooh' and 'coo' at, yet the constant haggling can wear even the most silver-tongued shopaholic down. By far the best way to haggle is with a smile on your face – a knowing wink and a sign that you're enjoying the process will go a lot further than a combative or mean-spirited stance. (The same goes for dealing with Moroccans in general; the most fundamentalist faces are often just furry facades for a surprisingly great sense of humour.)

When haggling we suggest starting at around one-third of the price that you are initially quoted and ending up at about 50%. Of course this is only a guide, not a hard and fast rule: some stores already offer fair prices, which is why some research prior to buying – if you have time of course – is a good idea. Even then, you still might end up over-paying, but at least you'll be close to a good price. Be aware, too, that no matter how low the price you achieve, it's very unlikely it'll be a huge bargain as Moroccans are all too aware of the real value of their goods. If it really looks like all is lost and you can't get the price you want, stop price-jousting and walk away. If your bartering partner doesn't call you back, chances are your requested price really was too low. Nine times out of ten, however, they'll wave you back and accept the final offer.

As for antiques, the majority are simply not authentic. We have listed some of the more genuine stores below and we recommend you try to verify any others you might come across before buying, either through your hotel/riad owner or perhaps a trusted personal shopper – one that doesn't accept commissions, of course (see Tour Guides and Personalized Services, page 182).

If you simply don't like haggling, tootle along to one of the artisans' centres listed below where prices are fixed (or as fixed as they're going to get in Morocco). In fact, it might be an idea to visit one of these before the souks, to get an idea of the average price of things.

As well as traditional goods, Marrakech also excels in turning out vast quantities of chic wares. Thanks largely to the designer ex-pat boom, stylish boutiques can be found dotted around the Medina (Kulchi, El Jouli, Beldi), Gueliz and out in the Palmeraie and industrial quarter (Sidi Ghanem). Shopping in these spots is vastly different. Strolling along the boulevards of Gueliz is like shopping at home, with a plethora of home furnishing stores, clothing shops, art galleries, large antique basements and just about everything else you can think of. There is generally no haggling here (prices are often on display), but nor is there much atmosphere, especially when compared with the souks.

Many of the exclusive villas in the Palmeraie and on the various routes out of the city – Jnane Tamsna, Palais Rhoul and the Amanjena, for example – have in-house boutiques, many of them selling excellent quality clothing and jewellery and so on, at expensive prices. It's a hike to get out to these spots but many also provide excellent lunches, health spas and sometimes even pool or tennis courts, so make an afternoon of a trip out here.

One of the least likely but assuredly rewarding areas to head for is Sidi Ghanem, Marrakech's industrial quarter, a 20-minute jaunt from the Jemaa el Fna. The main drag here – dubbed 'Rodeo Drive' by locals – scores a high minus on the aesthetic front but plays host to a range of wonderful warehouses offering quality goods at sweet prices. Our choices are Amira (candles), Akkal (ceramics), Via Notti (bed linen) and Fan Wa Nour (furniture/home accessories). Taxis cost 50dh to get out here but it's worth hiring one to stay with you for the duration of your shopping tour, as there are none to be found in this remote area. 200dh is a reasonable price to offer a driver for an hour.

Hours of shopping are fluid. In general, places seem to be open between 9am and 8pm daily in the souks, closed on Sundays in Gueliz and only open by appointment in the Palmeraie – but there are plenty of exceptions to these rules. It's always best to check the times for each individual store, although the souks especially are a law unto themselves: we found that even some of the times given to us directly by individual stores had to be taken with a pinch of salt, as proprietors often exercise their right to open and close when they want, particularly when the weather is unbearably hot, or on holy days, for example.

Note that there is no provision for tourists to reclaim any sales tax or VAT on accommodation or goods that they buy. Most of the places listed below accept credit cards although a few of the smaller ones in the souks don't. It's always best to carry some cash, just in case.

El Badil, 54 boulevard Moulay Rachid, Gueliz

Tel: 0 24 43 16 93

Open: 9am–7pm daily

El Badil offers only the most authentic antiques. You can find a glittering display of ancient treasures, arranged over two floors, that include Fez ceramics, Berber doors, mirrors, rugs, carpets, chests… and the list goes on. Brad Pitt and Hillary Clinton are just two of the flood of celebs who have popped their heads in, although it's a surprisingly down-to-earth place.

Galerie Mourjana, 33/2 Fhal Chaidmi Mouassine, Medina

Tel: 0 61 55 17 25

Open: 9am–noon, 3pm–8pm daily

Situated on a corner of the rue Mouassine, Galerie Mourjana is easy to find. It's a one-man show and refreshingly small in relation to the normal Ali Baba's Cave-style antique shop that seems to prevail in Marrakech. It offers a considered range of antiques, from chunky chests and tall candlesticks to Berber doors, silver teapots and myriad other curiosities. Prices are very reasonable and the owner is straightforward.

L'Orientalist, 11 and 15 rue de la Liberté, Gueliz

Tel: 0 24 43 40 74 F: 0 24 43 04 43 orientaliste@wanadoo.net.ma

Open: 9am–12.30pm, 3–7.30pm Mon–Sat; 10am–12.30pm Sun

L'Orientalist boasts a vast selection of modern and antique goods (it works with over a hundred local artisans) across two stores, located just along the road from one another. The larger shop holds most of the outsized delights, but between them they offer all kinds of artistic creations, paintings, perfumes, antiques, ceramics, marble, wood, enamelled glassware, textiles, clothes, cushions, plus modern clothing and designs and much more. A must for all budding designers.

La Porte d'Orient, 9 boulevard Mansour Eddahbi, Gueliz
Tel: 0 24 43 89 67
Open: 9am–7.30pm. Closed Sundays.

At first sight this place looks like every other antique shop, but make an appointment with the owner and you'll be shown a huge back room full of very genuine – and very expensive – antique artefacts. The front store specializes in wood but has jewellery, lamps, manuscripts, thrones and fountains to boot.

ART GALLERIES

Gallerie Bleu, 119 avenue Mohammed V, Gueliz
Tel: 0 24 42 00 80 g.bleue@menara.ma
Open: 10am–1pm, 4–8pm. Closed Mondays.

A recently opened space, small but fresh, Le Gallerie Bleu is the project of local artist Chalal, who displays his own semi-abstract daubings amid those of other Moroccan and international artists. Chalal is of Berber origin, a fact represented in his symbolist paintings that blend traditional religious motifs with Miró-esque shapes and colours.

Marrakech Arts Gallery, 60 boulevard Mansour, Gueliz
Tel: 0 24 43 93 41 www.art-gallery.marrakech.com
Open: 9am–1pm, 3–8pm daily

This place is the sister gallery of La Qoubba and exhibits primarily the same stuff – a predictable run of traditional paintings with little space retained for more interesting modern material.

Matisse Gallery, 61 rue de Yougoslavie, 43 Passage Ghandouri, Gueliz

Tel: 0 24 44 83 26 www.matisse-art-gallery.com
Open: 9.30am–1pm, 4–8pm daily

The Matisse Gallery is a space dedicated to showcasing both old and modern Moroccan artists. It is owned and carefully maintained by Youssef Falaki and Youssef Nabil Moroccan (both artists themselves) and has several

up-and-coming young artists on commission who have built up an impressive selection of lively, hip canvases. A refreshing change from the ubiquitous Orientalist works.

ARTISANS' MARKETS

Centre Artisanal, 7 Derb Baissi, Kasbah, Medina

Tel: 0 24 38 18 53/19 73 tapisantiquite@iam.net.ma
Open: daily, 8.30am–8pm

Located just along the road from the Saadian tombs, this is one of the most popular shopping spots and certainly one of the biggest. A vast, impersonal space, it stocks literally everything you could think of: handwoven rugs, Berber jewellery, antiques, teapots, home and garden furnishings, slippers, suitcases, kaftans and bejewelled daggers. It's soulless but convenient, and although it says no haggling, 'discounts' are available, especially if you buy a few items.

Centre Commercial, 3 Residence El Habib, 65 boulevard El Mansour Eddahbi, Gueliz
Tel: 0 24 43 92 58
Open: 9am–7pm daily

Centre Commercial is a large space choc-full of assorted goods. It's not as well known as the other two and doesn't seem to stock quite so much, but prices are more negotiable and there are still plenty of useful purchases to be had. The staff do occasionally try to fleece their customers, however, so be aware.

Ensemble Artisanal, avenue Mohammed V, MGueliz
Tel: 0 24 38 67 58
Open: 8.30am–7.30pm daily

Similar in style and appearance to the Centre Artisanal, this place sells a comparable range of goods and products (that is, everything from antique guns to leather suitcases). The added allure of the Ensemble is that it's state-owned, so all the products on display are supposedly there by royal decree and thus the best of their kind. It's also closer to the Jemaa el Fna than the other fixed-price craft shops.

BOUTIQUES

Akbar Delights, 45 Place Bab Fteuh, Medina
Tel: 0 71 66 13 07
Open: 11am–1pm, 3–9pm daily

Perhaps the most upmarket – certainly one of the most expensive – bou-
tiqes in the souks, Akbar Delights is pristine in its choice of imported luxury
fabrics from Kasmir and India and locally made garments, footwear and
accessories. Tucked away in a corner to the sprawling Place Egg Fteuh it's
yet another surprise find for most people, but the glittering array of scarves,
baboush, jewellery and assorted other clothing and accessories, while not
cheap, won't fail to impress.

Amanjena Boutiques, route de Ouarzazate, Km12
Tel: 0 24 40 33 53
Open: 8am–9pm daily

There are three boutiques at the luxurious Amanjena hotel, all selling wonderful designer clothes, fabrics, jewellery and candles by the likes of Valerie
Barkowski (of Mia Zia fame), Bridgette Perkins and Amina. It's a long way to
go, but you might also like to visit the hotel's spa, lunch at the poolside
restaurant (see EAT) or simply admire the opulent architecture. Booking
ahead for the spa and restaurant is essential.

Atelier Moro, 114 Place de Mouassine, Medina
Tel: 0 24 39 16 78   ateliermoro@menara.ma
Open: 9am–1pm; 3–7pm, Closed Tuesdays.

Owned by Viviana Gonzalez (of Riad El Fenn fame, see SLEEP), this cosy boutique, at the entrance to the dyer's souk, is marked by an anonymous wooden door and a number. Rap on the door and Viviana or her assistant Hadia will appear and invite you into a treasure-trove of one-off pieces and top-quality finds from all over Morocco and the world. Here be beach wraps from Sri Lanka, leather bags designed by Viviana herself, shell necklaces from southern Morocco and a smattering of own-label clothing. Those with a taste for individuality will want to hunt this place out.

Beldi, 9–11 Soukiat Laksour, Bab Fteuh, Medina
Tel: 0 24 44 10 76
Open: 9.30am–1pm, 3.30pm–8pm daily

Beldi is one of the best-known boutique outlets in the city, even if its scruffy exterior may suggest otherwise. Owned by two Moroccan brothers, it specializes in subtly westernized Moroccan cuts for men and women, in a range of compelling colours and magical materials. Collections change constantly so drop by to see what they have on offer.

Boutique Indigo, Palais Rhoul, route de Fes, Palmeraie
Tel: 0 61 30 73 33 (Fanny)
Open: by appointment only

The Palais Rhoul's in-house boutique is slightly different from other Palmeraie spots in that it avoids the Pink City vogue for Euro–Marrakchi designer hybrids and instead offers a full selection of western clothing brands. The sizeable store offers bags, sweaters, jeans, jackets and shoes ranging from smart to casual and made by the likes of Pinko, American Retro, Calvin Klein and Miss June. Prices are more or less what you'd pay in Europe, but it's the only place you'll find these kinds of clothes and accessories in town. The shop is happily located right beside the Palais' swish L'Abyssin restaurant (see EAT) and is a short stroll from the best *hammam* and spa in town (see PLAY).

Creation et Passementerie, 2 Souk el Kimakhine, Medina

Tel: 0 24 44 04 98 yalaoui63@hotmail.com

Open: 10am–9pm. Closed Fridays.

If you're looking for cute women's clothing/accessories made from sabra – that stuff that looks like silk but is cheaper – then this spot could be for you. Owner Youssef El Alaoui won a magazine award for Most Innovative Moroccan Designer in 2005 and has kept on introducing interesting designs ever since. Hard to find, but worth the effort, his shop boasts an ever-changing assortment of pretty, colourful accessories with a local twist: tassled key-rings and garments as well as a medley of bras, belts and bracelets on display across two floors. It's one of the few places in the souk with air-conditioning.

Kulchi, 1 bis, Moul Laksour (opposite the Laksour Fountain), Marrakech

Tel: 0 62 64 97 83 kulchimarrakech@hotmail.com

Open: 9.30am–1pm, 4–8pm. Closed Sundays.

A cute little space if ever there was one, Kulchi is half-hidden away just along from a herbalist's on the corner of rue Mouassine. Inside are coolly contemporary clothes, bags and accessories with an antique twist, as well as jewellery, T-shirts, shoes, perfumes and vintage *djellabahs*. Pricey but lovely, Kulchi is one of the Medina's more consistent and well-known outlets.

Meryanne Loum-Martin Boutique, Jnane Tamsna, Douar Abiad, La Palmeraie

Tel: 0 24 32 94 23 www.jnanetamsna.com

Open: 10am–10pm daily (by appointment only)

Meryanne Loum-Martin is one of Marrakech's more established design entities. Her showroom used to be situated in the Medina but has now moved out to her delightful villa in the Palmeraie (see Jnane Tamsna, Sleep/Eat). As well as an array of her own innovative designs, Meryanne's boutique showcases the work of other known designers such as silk-scarf creator Paige Hathaway-Thorn. Think hand-woven *djellabahs*, cool kaftans, jewellery, purses, china, home accessories, paintings, old photos, smooth raffia and cotton,

157

cushions, bedclothes, stylish baboush and many other things that squeak with chic. Lunch here is recommended.

Michele Baconnier, 6 rue de Vieux, Gueliz

Tel: 0 24 44 91 78 michelebaconnier@yahoo.fr
Open: 9am 1pm, 3pm–7pm. Closed Sundays.

Compact and bijou, Paris-based Michele Baconnier's boutique is well worth a peek. Known for merging the traditional and the hip in ever-interesting ways, her Marrakech outlet stocks a range of cool jewellery, clothing, *baboush*, handbags, candlesticks, rugs and soaps. There are some antiques to be found here too (furnishings as well as clothing) and although the tiny pavement café has now sadly closed, there is a new spa, Beldi, located just along the road (see PLAY).

Milouad El Jouli, Souk Smat El Marga 6–8, Medina

Tel: 0 24 42 67 16 / 0 70 41 76 61 meljouli@hotmail.com
Open: 10am–6pm daily

Girls who like Hermes are going to love Milouad El Jouli. This hip little space employs local artisans to create all kinds of fabulous women's things – bags, baboush, smocks, sandals, heavy belts – designed by the owner, who does a great line in Hermes-a-likes. Most of the things here have a Moroccan twist, especially the clothes, which are lovely but might not look so natural in Soho. Everything is immaculately made and while prices aren't cheap, they do reflect the quality and the owners tend to be fair. A larger shop is set to open just around the corner; ask here for more details.

CARPETS AND RUGS

Art Akhnif, 6 Fhal chidmi Mouassine, Medina

Tel: 0 24 42 60 96 artakhnif@hotmail.com
Open: 9am–8pm daily

There are many rug and carpet sellers in the Medina, but this family-run joint is one of the more comfortable spaces to get acquainted with the splendid array of Morocco's hand-woven goods. The owners are professional and fair people with a good knowledge of what is and what isn't worth money. The downstairs boasts all kinds of colourful Berber classics and other interesting weaves at very reasonable prices, while an upstairs section lies in wait for those who'd like to get a little more serious. You can pick up some genuine antiques here.

Bazaar les Palmiers, 145 Souk Dakkakine, Medina
Tel: 0 24 44 46 29
Open: 9am–7pm. Closed Fridays.

Run by the friendly, English-speaking Hamid, this cosy little spot offers an array of wonderfully coloured carpets, cushions and rugs, mostly hailing from the High Atlas region. There's a mix of antiques and contemporary goods, and while it's not the cheapest, everything is in respectable condition and seems fairly priced.

FOOTWEAR

Ahmed Ait Taleb, 236 Souk El Kebire, Medina
Tel: 0 24 40 58 88 / 0 70 40 45 02 / 0 70 57 10 25
Open: 9.30am–6.30pm daily

There are gazillions of stores selling *baboush* in the Medina, but Ahmed's is in the top 10% when it comes to comfort and even style and finish. Here you can find a variety of men and women's shoes and sandals, made from leather, nubuck and suede, and ranging from the sequinned and the stripy to the curly of toe and the open-toed. It's the soft, slipper-like interiors that really work for us, though, as well as Ahmed's reliably upfront method of dealing with customers.

Atika, 34 rue de la Liberté, Gueliz
Tel: 0 24 43 64 09 www.atikaboutique.com
Open: 8.30am–12.30pm, 3–7.30pm. Closed Sundays.

There is another Atika in town (down the road at 212 Mohammed V), but this is the biggest and most popular. It does a fine line in chic and stylish footwear (shoes, boots, sandals, sneakers, and so on, for men and women) in a range of local and international styles.

HOME DECORATION

Amira, Z.I. Sidi Ghanem Industrial Estate
Tel: 0 24 33 62 47 www.amirabougies.com
Open: 9am–1pm, 2.30–6pm. Closed Sundays.

Amira is by far the classiest candle store in town. The candles here are renowned internationally and grace many a romantic Moroccan setting. They come in an assortment of shapes, sizes and colours and are laid out in a spacious warehouse that shows them at their best. Amira is close to other stores such as Akkal and Via Notti (see below).

Artisan El Koutoubia, 54 bis, Fhel Chidmi Mouassine, Medina
Tel: 0 24 44 46 09 artkoutoubia@hotmail.com
Open: 9am–6pm daily

Artisan El Koutoubia is an organized and pretty little lamp shop that may appeal to those who prefer not to indulge in base haggling for illumination. The styles on display are similar to many in the souks – nothing truly exciting – but the space is more given to browsing and the staff are a little more professional.

Casa Mangani, 26 rue Tarik Ibn Zyad, Gueliz
Tel: 0 24 43 56 34 www.mangani.net
Open: 9am–1pm, 3.30–7.30pm. Closed Sundays and Monday afternoons.

If you don't know the famous Florentine porcelain called Mangani, you will after coming here. The shop is full of lamps made from the stuff, pleasantly displayed throughout a happening little show-space. The designs tend to teeter between Italian and Moroccan, and vary in shape, size and pattern, but are mostly ornamental. What might prove more eye-catching for the minimalists are the furniture designs of architect/designer Soumaya Jalal, who works with raffia, horse-hair and other materials to produce low-key stylish wall-hangings, cushions, curtains and rugs in pleasing whites, coffees and creams.

Fan Wa Nour 16 Z.I Sidi Ghanem, Marrakech
Tel: 0 24 33 69 60
Open: 9.30–1pm, 2–6pm. Closed Sundays & Monday mornings.

Don't be put off by the NCP feel of Fna Na Wour's charmless façade. To ascend and enter the third floor of this building in the Sidi Ghanem industrial district is to be exposed to a world of uber-stylish home decoration created by the warehouse's Belgian owner and several other European artists. The space holds a cool miscellany of goods made from myriad materials; beds wrought from iron, tables carved from wood, lamps wrangled from leather. Sizes and prices vary from the large and expensive to the small and quite expensive. Not a spot for budget shoppers then, but a must for seekers of sleek, contemporary one-off home furnishings.

Hassan Makchad, Souk Shkayria 161, Medina
Tel: 0 70 72 52 84
Open: 9am–7pm. Closed Fridays.

Hassan's stall is not the easiest spot to find in the souks, but it's certainly not the hardest either. It's an itsy space that stocks cute, well turned-out accessories crafted from good calibre leather. If you're after cheap but well-made, unique gifts such as leather-clad notebooks and leather photo frames, jewellery boxes in the shape of drums and lovely purses in bright, satisfying colours, this is a good option.

Jamade, Riad Zitoun Jdid, 1 place Douar Graoua, Medina
Tel: 0 24 42 90 42   hotelriadcelia@yahoo.fr
Open: 10am–1.15pm, 3–8pm daily

Just along the well-traversed Riad Zitoun Jdid and located right next door to the Riad Celia (to which it is connected), Jamade is an elegant surprise in a street full of mediocre knick-knack shops. An immediately attractive space, it sells gorgeous little accessories such as purses, slippers, jewellery, plates, handbags, candles, photographs and cook-books. Everything is crafted by local artisans and has a trendy slant.

Kif Kif, 8 rue des Ksour, Bab Laksour, Medina
Tel: 0 61 08 20 41
Open: 9.30pm–1.30pm, 2.30–7.30pm daily

If you visit just one knick-knack store in Marrakech, make it Kif Kif, one of the best-known miscellany stores in the Medina. Not everything here rocks, but the majority does. While away lovely minutes here sorting through belts and bags, bangles and candles, table crockery, lamps, dressing-gowns and even a smattering of clothing for kids. Kif Kif isn't inside the souks either, making it a better shopping experience for claustrophobes.

Original Design, 47 place des Ferblantiers, Medina

Tel: 0 24 38 03 61 Original_design_mrk@yahoo.fr
Open: 9am–7.30pm. Closed noon–2pm and Wednesdays.

A pretty jewel amid the rough and clangorous environs of the place des Ferblantiers, Original Design is the creation of Mademoiselle Ibtissam Ait Daoud. She has fitted out this small but very sweet space with her choice of crockery, embroidered materials, mirrors, soaps, *tajine* pots, placemats, candles and other lovely knick-knacks. Prices are reasonable, she accepts commissions, and can export bulk buys to Europe if you get really carried away. There's another shop around the corner on the Riad Zitoun Jdid that stocks similar goods in different colours.

Scenes du Lin, 70 rue de la Liberté, Gueliz

Tel: 0 24 43 61 08 bleumajorelle@menara.ma
Open: 9.30am–12.30pm, 3.30–7.30pm. Closed Sundays.

Scenes du Lin is a striking, low-lit store run by French textile expert Anna-Marie Chaoui and her Moroccan husband. The original function of this place was as a showroom for her wonderful collection of natural fabrics, some of which, like *mlifr*, are local, while others are imported from around the world. The place also sells tablecloths, dressing-gowns, curtains, kaftans and bed-spreads, plus snazzy furnishings and funky candles made by Laurence Corsin and Amira, respectively.

Via Notti, 322 Sidi Ghanem, Route De Safi

Tel: 0 24 35 60 24
Open: 9am–6pm Closed Sundays.

Climb the flight of stairs to the left of Akkal (as you are facing it) to arrive at Via Notti and a soft, seductive world of all things bed- and bathroom-related. It's a light, airy space that offers the anticipated stock of pillowcases, bedsheets, duvet covers, bath-robes and towels and other relevant bits and bobs. Designs run from the ornate to the minimal, but all with some kind of local twist. It's disappointing that the store doesn't offer any additional options in terms of fabrics – what you see is what you get, which means you must like white to shop here – though the embroidery and designs are open to discussion.

Yahya, No 49–51 Passage Ghandouri, off Rue de Yougoslavie, Gueliz
Tel: 0 24 42 27 76 www.yahyacreation.com
Open: 10am–12.30pm, 2.30–7pm. Closed Sundays.

If it's contemporary decorative objects or furniture you're after in brass and other metals, Yahya probably won't disappoint. Run by English born Yahya, the designs here are traditional Moroccan artisan but with a clean, contemporary edge, and the quality and feel of the products are second to none. Many of the pieces are alarmingly large. Having recently won a prestigious award in the yearly Riad Expo show, he is very popular among locals and internationals alike: his client list includes Harrods. The showroom is worth visiting for its cool ambience alone; a brand new space is planned for next door.

HOME FURNISHINGS

Ambiance & Styles, rue de la Liberté, Gueliz
Tel: 0 24 43 71 11
Open: 9.30am–12.30pm, 3.30–7.30pm. Closed Sundays.

The project of two Moroccan women – manager Ouafa El Idrissi and designer Siham Tazi – Ambiance & Styles is an immediately eye-catching store. Gawp through the window and feast on an eclectic collection of large home furnishings ranging from sofas, tables, beds and cabinets to accessories such as candles, covers and throws, lamps, bean bags, cushions. It's all done with a funky/retro/art deco twist that runs from the slightly kitsch to the impeccably cool. The only drawback is that the shop doesn't offer a shipping service, so getting any large items back home is left completely up to you.

Interieur 29, B29 rue Mansour Eddahbu, Gueliz
Tel: 0 24 43 31 12
Open 9.30am–12.15pm, 3.30–7pm. Closed Sundays and Monday afternoons.

Pascal Colombeau and Hubert Aimetti design furnishings of all kinds in styles such as Art Deco and the more linear look known to some as 'colonial'. They work in wood, iron, alloys and all kinds of fabrics to create refined bedspreads, chairs, bowls, table sets, chests and mirrors among a million other things. Everything is elegantly minimal and comes in de rigueur ethnic colours.

Les Lamps D'Aladin, 78–81 rue Mouassine, Medina
Tel: 0 66 15 56 69   kermous_youssef@yahoo.fr
Open: 9am–7pm daily

Lamps are big business in Marrakech and they come in myriad shapes and sizes. Despite the catch-all connotations of the name, Lamps D'Aladain is actually just a tiny store – literally a shack on rue Mouassine – that specializes in lamps made of bronze, silver and a hybrid of bronze and silver known as *maishor*. They tend to be robustly built and are available in a variety of sizes that are suitable for both home and garden.

Lun'Art Gallery, 24 rue Moulay Ali, Gueliz
Tel: 0 24 44 72 66   lunart@iam.net.ma
Open: 10am–12.30pm, 4–8pm. Closed Sundays.

Lun'Art has been run by Luciano (Italian) and Said (Moroccan) for 10 years and is well known in town. Luciano is the designer, and his furniture has been increasingly in demand since he opened, not only from the general public but also from props specialists (his work has appeared in locally filmed movies such as *The Mummy* and *Kundun*). Larger products (such as garden furniture) are on display outside, while the rest is shown around two big rooms inside the main building. There's a large ethnic and antique slant with such objects as Maori tables, Moroccan chairs and Balinese sculptures up for grabs.

Maison de Bali, Passage Ghandouri 34–35, 61 rue de Yougoslavie, Gueliz
Tel: 0 24 43 63 12 www.maisondebali.com
Open: 9am–7pm. Closed Sundays.

No prizes for guessing what this place specializes in. Aside from smart and expensive Balinese furnishings, however, Maison de Bali also stocks Moroccan goods and items from places such as Laos, Turkey and European countries. Some pieces here are predictable, some imaginative, others irresistible. There's an especially good line in beds, tables and funky lamps. A second store can be found at 165 avenue Mohammed V.

Ministero del Gusto, 22 Derb Azzouz El Mouassine (off rue Sidi El Yamami), Medina
Tel: 0 24 42 64 55 www.ministerodelgusto.com
Open: 10am–1pm, 4–7pm. Sundays by appointment only.

Designers Fabrizio Bizzarri and Alessandra Lippini (formerly style editor for Italian *Vogue*) opened their 'Ministry of Taste' a few years ago. It's a breathtaking space, a feast of curves, crazy artwork and imaginations gone wild.

Within the wilfully wobbly walls is a range of furnishings and decorations made by the owners and their designer and artist friends from around the world, who contribute pieces that are often as madly creative as the space that they inhabit. Three times a year the gallery hosts music and art exhibitions.

Mustapha Blaoui, rue Bab Doukkala 142–4, Medina
Tel: 0 24 38 52 40 tresordesnomades@hotmail.com
Open: 9am–8pm daily

This place must surely have been invented with the (possibly male) shop-a-phobe in mind. Set outside the bustling souks, just down the road from the Dar El Bacha (which handily serves as a taxi pick up/drop off point), Blaoui is a well-known one-stop shop for all kinds of traditional Moroccan goodies, from lamps and tea-chests to candlesticks, pottery and studded leather draws. There are a couple of rooms but much of the stock is stacked in the first large space you come into. Non-enthusiasts can lounge on a sofa and browse from a more or less horizontal position while sipping mint tea – or simply recline fully and leave the eager ones too it. Prices are fair, goods are quality and staff are helpful.

JEWELLERY

Bellawi, Kessariat Lossta 56, Souk El Attarin, Medina
Tel: 0 24 44 01 07
Open: 9am–7pm. Closed Fridays.

With family links to the masterfully miscellaneous Moustapha Blaoui (see PLAY), Bellawi is much smaller and more specialized, offering an in-depth selection of bracelets and bangles, necklaces and rings made from all kinds of materials, including beads and precious stones. It's a bit tricky to find but get close and ask for the owner Abdelatif, who is well known in these parts.

La Cabane d'Ali Baba, 53 rue de Commerce, Cartier Juif, Hay Essalam
Tel : 0 61 24 71 55
Open: 9am–7pm. Closed Fridays.

Not for the faint-hearted, this shop is literally crammed full of all types of beads, either on strings, or in fully formed necklaces. There are also kilim-covered baskets (also for sale) choc-full of hand-tooled metal pendants (from 8dh each) and assorted stones to be sold by weight. You need a bit of time here to really rummage around and fully savour the variety of objects available.

POTTERY AND CERAMICS

Akkal, 322 Sidi Ghanem, Route De Safi
Tel: 0 24 33 59 38
Open: 8am–6pm (5pm Sat). Closed Sundays.

Ceramic sophisticates will not want to leave this space once they've stepped inside. Neither will baby-clothes lovers, garment/fabric aficionados or art collectors, since Belgian designer Charlotte has transformed her warehouse into a showroom not just for herself but for others too, such as Valerie Barkowski (of Mia Zia fame) and other local artful types. It's one of the most attractive retail spots in the city, with a lay-out designed to keep you constantly hooked with an array of gorgeously crafted designer products and dazzling colours. If you get really carried away Akkal arranges overseas shipping.

Art & Deco (Chez Alaoui), rue Molkssour Sabet Graoua 52, Medina
Tel: 0 64 95 64 35 (Hafid) / 0 62 08 48 71 (Mourad)
Open: 9am–8pm daily

Ever seen those seductive, dark-green coloured ceramics around in the Medina and wondered where they come from and what the name is? No? Well, we'll tell you anyway: the pieces are called Ceramic Du Tamgrout and they hail from – surprise, surprise – the city of Tamgrout in the south. This small store stocks lots of it in the shape of bowls, lamps, dishes, cups and other bits and bobs. There are other colours and types of crockery here too that may interest kitchen connoisseurs.

Pottery Souk, Boulevard du Golf, Souk Rbiaa, SYBA, Medina
Open: 8am–7pm daily

If it's traditional pottery you seek – decorated or plain – then this large, shop-lined boulevard souk is for you. Tajine pots, mini-Koutoubias, vases,

flowerpots, decorative objects and suchlike are all stacked up outside the premises in higgledy-piggledy fashion. Some of the stores will be happy to let you see how *zellije* tables or *tadelakt* lamps are made, if you're interested.

TRADITIONAL CLOTHING

Azziza, Centre Commercial Liberté, rue de la Liberté, Gueliz
Tel: 0 24 44 98 73
Open: 8am–12.30pm, 3–7.30pm daily

Azziza is a Moroccan designer who makes prêt-à-porter garments for men and women, although there is a bias towards women's wear. The shop stocks something for every occasion, from smart suits to leather jackets and casual *djellabahs*. A lot of Azziza's designs are high quality if stylistically ordinary, but there are some experimental gems to be found.

Galerie Birkemeyer, 169 rue Mohammed El Bekal, Gueliz

Tel: 0 24 44 69 63 www.iam.net.ma/birkemeyer

Open: 8.30am–12.30pm, 3–7.30pm. Closed Sunday afternoons.

A large store just off the Boulevard Zouktouni famed for its selection of leather and suede clothing and accoutrements. The staff look on somewhat balefully while you rummage through everything from jackets, trousers, handbags, luggage and non-leather items such as scarves and shirts. Not especially funky, and not overly cheap, but the quality is good.

La Maison du Kaftan Morocain, 65 rue Sidi El Yamani, Mouassine, Medina

Tel: 0 24 44 10 51

Open: 8am–7pm daily

As the name suggests, this shop specializes in traditional kaftans. In fact, if you can't find the kaftan you're looking for in here, then it probably exists only in your own mind, or in fashion haunts such as Kulchi or Jnane Tamsna. The shop front leads into a vast room around which are hung kaftans of all colours and sizes: antique kaftans, Berber kaftans – even magic kaftans! There are also other traditional accessories such as baboush, chemises and pantaloons, for men and women.

TRADITIONAL HANDICRAFTS

Bijouterie El Yasmine Abdelghani, 68 Riad Zaitoun Jdid, Medina
Open: 9am–6pm daily

The elderly chap that runs this small spot makes the most exquisite hand-tooled necklaces and cutlery out of resin and wood. He sells them to only a couple of traders in the souk, but for the best quality and variety try and locate the man himself. His dainty teaspoons are 25dh each (unless you buy in bulk, when the price is reduced considerably) and there are also paper knives, dessert forks and salad servers all made in unusual and beautiful styles.

Kainkila Bougage (Chez Sidammed), Fhal Chidmi Rue Lamoissine, Kissariat Lamoisni, Medina
Tel: 0 62 01 34 11 / 0 65 12 80 89 / 0 24 44 35 00
Open: 9am–6pm daily

Actually a series of three shops rather than one, this is the place to come if you are interested not in Moroccan handicrafts but in ornaments and accessories hand-made by Sub-Saharan tribes. The owners Sidammed and Azziz are both Touareg people but speak incredibly good English and happily impart interesting knowledge about the people who make the works they sell. Wooden masks, brass and jewellery, antiques, rugs, outsized vases… you can find pretty much everything here, all one-offs and hand-made, and they serve refreshing mint tea.

play...

If you consider Marrakech to be a little underwhelming in the sightseeing department, the vast range of activities it has to offer is more than compensatory, especially if you're willing to venture outside the city.

The more actively inclined can ascend Mount Toubkal, hike around the Atlas Mountains, wind-surf in Essouira and even ski and snowboard if conditions are right (usually between January and March). Less demanding, but just as much fun, are the city's horse-riding schools, and the go-karting and quad-biking courses.

Sports enthusiasts might enjoy a round or two of golf (there are three courses that host domestic and international championships), or perhaps some tennis, pigeon-shooting, swimming or squash. Head out towards the desert, and camel-riding, dune-climbing and 4x4 exploration safaris become an option.

Those wishing to stay closer to home can enjoy the city's expansive spa and *hammam* scene. A *hammam* ('spreader of warmth') is a traditional form of

personal cleansing that can trace its roots back to Roman baths. It consists of being steamed and washed down with soap then drubbed by a man or woman sporting a mitt with a texture like a Brillo-pad (a 'gommage'). This is sometimes followed (depending on the type of hammam you choose) by the application of lavender, rose water, a face-mask or shampoo.

Marrakech can be a hectic and draining place. If you're staying for longer than three days you might find it beneficial to get out of the city and see some of the surrounding area. Three different places immediately spring to mind. First of all, there's the Kasbah du Toubkal (see page 183) set in the shadow of Jebel Toubkal, the highest mountain in the High Atlas. The Kasbah is in a stunning location with spectacular views, and to get there you drive through the orchards of Asni. You can lunch here, visit the Berber villages, wander the mountain trails or simply relax with a hammam.

Next, the Kasbah Agafay (page 174) is one of the few places that allow visitors to use their pool. Cooking courses, an extensive spa, good food and a great

setting make the trip well worthwhile. Lastly, just a little further on from the Kasbah, is La Pause (page 184), a surreally beautiful spot in the Agafay Desert that offers solitude, cycling, trekking, horse-riding and even a spot of crazy golf.

COOKERY SCHOOLS

Morocco's natural pantry is a genuine joy, with fresh fruit and vegetables, spices and flavours in healthy abundance. If you wander the earthier side of the Medina the scent of mint and other fresh herbs fills the air, or head out of the city in the autumn and the aroma of apples and pears pervades. Mix this with a unique form of cuisine, and you'll not be surprised learn that there is an exciting range of cooking schools in the city.

Dar Liqama, Douar Abiad, Palmeraie
Tel: 0 24 33 16 97 www.darliqama.com

In October and November the luxury Palmeraie villa Dar Liqama hosts the internationally renowned Rhodes School of Cuisine. The Moroccan course is a week long, and guests get to enjoy the villa's full facilities – spa, *hammam*, tennis courts, movie room included.

Kasbah Agafay, Route de Guemassa, Km 20
Tel: 0 24 36 86 00 www.kasbahagafay.com

Set in a stunning kasbah with beautiful views over the desert, fields and the High Atlas, the Agafay boasts a stunning location for a cookery school. Its garden provides all the fresh vegetables, fruits and herbs you need. Go just for the day course, or stay overnight and wallow in luxury and sophistication.

La Maison Arabe, 1 Derb Assehbe, Bab Doukkala, Medina
Tel: 0 24 38 70 10 www.lamaisonarabe.com

This exclusive Medina hotel has a cookery school based out in the Palmeraie for the use of its guests. Coupled with the use of a swimming pool, it makes for a therapeutic and fun day out.

Souk Cusine, Zniquat Rahba, Derb Tahtah 5
Tel: 0 73 80 49 55 www.soukcuisine.com

Run by Gemma Van de Burgt, who is Dutch, this dedicated cooking school starts at 11am and lasts for three hours. Gemma favours small groups (four max) to allow for ingredient-shopping in the souks, although on Mondays and Thursdays she can cater for larger groups.

GOLF

Golf in Morocco is surprisingly popular, and there are no fewer than three international courses located just outside the city. Courses are generally easy to get on to and relatively cheap compared with European prices – green fees start at around 300dh, caddies around 90dh. Of course, the weather is more or less guaranteed 300 days of the year.

Golf d'Amelkis, Route de Ouarzazate, Km 12, Marrakech
Tel: 0 24 40 44 14
Open: 7am–6pm daily in summer, 7.30am–3.30pm in winter

Amelkis is the newest kid on the block, and it shows. It's the best-looking course around (designed by Cabell B. Robinson) and boasts an elegant and relaxing clubhouse and professional on-site shop, which sells everything from tees to T-shirts. A round will set you back 500dh, the green costs 700dh a day, and caddies and golf carts can be hired.

Palmeraie Golf Palace, Palmeraie
Tel: 0 24 30 10 10 www.pgp.co.ma
Open: 7am–7pm daily

Designed by international maestro Robert Trent Jones, this is the pride and joy – and the principal *raison d'être* – of the vast PGP estate. It's a classic American-style course with seven lakes, lots of palm trees and a very nice clubhouse and restaurant. Lessons can be arranged, and clubs can be rented for 25dh each or 250dh for the whole bag. Eighteen holes will set you back 450dh, with a whole day on the course stretching you to 600dh. For ultimate decadence a local caddy can be arranged for 80dh.

Royal Golf Club, Ancienne Route de Ouarzazate Km 2, Marrakech
Tel: 0 24 40 98 28 Royal_golf@iam.net.ma
Open: Sunrise–sunset daily in summer, 7.30am–2.30pm in winter

The oldest and most regal of courses in Marrakech, this course is quite flat, and set in a dense forest of cypress, eucalyptus and palm trees, overlooked by the Atlas Mountains. Many of Morocco's more famous visitors have had a game here and lessons are given all year round. The clubhouse, new sports shop and bar have recently been constructed and are open from 8am until 6pm. Green fees are 450dh for the day, 18 holes is 400dh and clubs can be hired for 250dh a bag.

HORSE-RIDING

Marrakech has a variety of places where you can jump into the saddle. They are professionally run even if some look very basic, usually offering lessons, hacking and jumping, and catering for children as well as adults. All the places listed have paddocks of differing sizes, but also suggest trips around the countryside or into the mountains. The countryside around Marrakech is not incredibly exciting, so you might like to arrange for the stables to meet you with horses in the mountains. Most stables will offer you trekking options with accommodation, so that you can spend up to four or five days riding outdoors.

Cavalier Ranch, Route de Fes, Km 14, Marrakech
Tel: 0 62 61 22 51 cavalierranch@menara.ma
Open: 8.30am–7pm. Closed Mondays.
Prices: Horses 100dh per hour, 600dh per day

Run by the oddly charming Gallaoui, this place is a little further out than the others but nevertheless worth it. The horses are Berber and Arabic; you can jump or trot round the paddocks, tour the local villages or organize a longer-distance trip into the mountains or the desert (which includes food and accommodation).

Club Equestre de la Palmeraie, Palmeraie Golf Palace, Palmeraie
Tel: 0 24 36 87 93 www.pgp.co.ma
Open: daily, 8am–noon, 3–8pm in summer; 8am–noon, 3–6pm in winter
Prices: horses 150dh per hour, 800dh per day; ponies 50dh per 15mins, 90dh per hour

---

The Golf Palace's stables are relatively small but probably the prettiest of the lot. There's a paddock that's used mainly for beginners and children, while accomplished riders can roam around the desert villages of the Palmeraie. The Palace has many other facilities nearby, including a hotel, should you want to spend some more time here.

La Roseraie, Ouirgane
Tel: 0 24 43 91 28/9

La Roseraie is a country hotel with horse-riding facilities located 60km from Marrakech (in the Ouirgane Valley). The advantage of coming all the way here is that you are already in the foothills of the Atlas Mountains with easy access to forests, reserves, hamlets and Berber villages where you can ride and trek. Horses can be ridden by the hour or you can disappear into the countryside for up to five nights, staying at Berber houses en route. The hotel has plenty of pleasant rooms, a fine restaurant, a full health spa and 50 acres of garden to relax in.

Royal Club Equestre de Marrakech, Route d'Amizmiz, Km 4, Marrakech
Tel: 0 24 38 18 49
Open: 8am–noon, 2–6pm. Closed Mondays.

This state-run stable is perhaps the main centre in town – it's certainly the most official. There are a couple of large paddocks here, and several different breeds of horse to choose from. It offers individual lessons or will organize treks of varying lengths to suit. The trainers are professional and national competitions are held here occasionally. Prices start from 150dh per hour for a horse, while children can get a 15-minute pony ride for 15dh.

QUAD BIKING AND KARTING

Atlas Karting, Route De Safi, Marrakech
Tel: 0 64 19 05 37/0 61 23 76 87 www.ilovemarrakesh.com/atlaskarting or atlas_karting@yahoo.fr
Open: 8am–7pm daily

Atlas Karting is run by a pro Frenchman by the name of Gerard. It offers a challenging and fun-packed course that karters of all levels are welcome to try out (lessons and seminars are available). Also on offer are day trips that allow enthusiasts to get to grips with both quads and karts (1,900dh), and there's camel-riding and horse-riding as well. A kart starts at 100dh for 10 minutes, while camels can be hired at 280dh for an hour. Facilities include a snack bar and a hotel.

Mega-Quad Excursions, Route d'Amizmiz, Km 6
Tel: 0 44 38 31 91/0 61 21 69 24 www.quadmaroc.com
Open: 8am–7pm daily

This is a neat little place with plenty of well-maintained quads, a tented restaurant on-site for lunches and special events, and a course that stretches across the local countryside. Trips to the mountains and the desert are available, and start at 2,000dh per day, including lunch, going up to 15,000dh (this pays for a minimum of six quads for five days, including accommodation).

SKIING

Oukaimeden Ski Resort
Information: 0 2 20 37 98

The place ski-buffs should head for is the city of Oukaimeden, 74km outside Marrakech and 3,273m above sea level. It's North Africa's largest ski resort, initially developed by the French and more recently surveyed by international resort planners who aim to improve the infrastructure. Lift passes are cheap, as is the equipment to hire, but an absence of snow can be a slight problem. Between mid-January and mid-February is the safest bet, although the views are great all year round. In good conditions there are up to 20km of runs, the longest of which is 3km. Donkeys can be hired to access terrain not served by lifts, which opens up some impressive steeps and chutes. Otherwise ski touring is available including an ascent/descent of Jebel Toubkal, North Africa's highest mountain.

SPAS AND HAMMAMS

Amanjena Spa, Route De Ouarzazate, Km 12

Tel: 0 24 403 353 www.amanresorts.com
Open: 8am–9pm daily
Prices: *hammam* 600dh (45 mins), massage 850dh (hour)

The Amanjena's exclusive-as-you-like Health and Beauty Centre offers *hammams*, steam baths, a glassed-in whirlpool and the full range of treatments from massages and manicures to pedicures and facials. There's also a timber floor fitness centre and a fantastic Thai restaurant (see page 74) that is fully recommended. Non-residents are not allowed to use the pool.

Bains de Marrakech, 2 Derb Sedra, Bab Agnaou, Medina

Tel: 0 24 38 14 28
Open: 9am–8pm daily

Bains de Marrakech, annexed to the delightful Riad Mehdi (see SLEEP), is one of the only places in town to offer extensive spa services in a non-corporate environment. Set in a *riad*, it boasts a delightful courtyard for relaxation, and dark, scented corridors off which are located various treatment rooms. You can get everything here from a facial and a feisty *hammam/gommage* to a four-hand massage and French manicure. There are also some luxurious bathing options, including one that incorporates milk, orange flowers, sensual oils and rose petals; two sunken baths positioned next to each other mean you can indulge with someone else, should you so desire. Day spas (3 hrs) and weekend packages are also available with prices starting at 150dh for a *hammam*, rising to 320dh for an hour-long massage.

Dar Attajmil, 23 rue Laksour (off rue Sidi El Yamami), Medina

Tel: 0 24 42 69 66 darattajmil@iam.net.ma
Prices: *hammam* 200dh, with massage 440dh

If you'd like a more intimate *hammam* experience, try Attajmil. The *riad* itself is small (five rooms) and the *hammam* on the roof is also compact, but it's sizeable enough, while the treatment is professional and rigorous, and includes right essential oils. Mint tea is included in the price, and the roof garden is a gorgeous place to sip it and unwind – day or night. They need at least 3 hours' notice to get the fire going and guests take preference, so booking ahead is essential.

Hammam Nikhil, Zohor 1, Ain Itti
Open: 6am–9.30pm daily

Local *hammams* in Marrakech can sometimes be run-down or downright unpleasant. Others, however, are newer, and manage to create a good balance of decent scrub-down, cleanliness and sociability. Nikhil is one such. It's basic – think bright lights and shiny tiled floors – but cheap and clean, and a great way of getting a direct insight into local social customs (many Marrakchi come here principally for a chinwag). As is customary, Nikhil has separate male and female sections and offers basic services from 7dh.

Les Jardins de la Medina, 21 Rue Derb Chtouka, Kasbah, Medina
Tel: 0 24 38 18 51 www.lesjardinsdelamedina.com
Open: 8.30am-8.30pm daily
Price: *hammams/gommage* and 30-minute massage 350dh

Les Jardins de la Medina does not have a spa complex as such, but does possess a *hammam* (downstairs near the swimming pool) and a health and beauty suite up on the roof, which offers haircuts, massages, facials and other assorted treatments. It's a little smaller than other *hammams*, and as the hotel's guests obviously take preference, it's worth a phone call in advance to book.

Palais Rhoul, Route de Fes, Dar Tounsi
Tel: 0 24 32 94 94/95 www.palaisrhoul.com
Prices: massage 650dh (1 hour), *hammam* 400dh

Listed amongst *Harper's* world top 100, the Palais Rhoul's extensive spa is oft-cited as the best in Marrakech. The *hammam* in particular is a unique experience, thanks to resident therapist Abdel Kader, who trained under his father in the ancient therapy form of *tkissila*. As well as the usual wash-down and scrub, Kader also administers bone-cracking and other techniques that leave you feeling more than incredible.

Les Secrets De Marrakech, 62 Rue De La Liberte, Gueliz
Tel: 0 24 43 48 48
Open: 10am–8pm. Closed Sundays.
Price: 250dh (30 min massage), 180–280dh (*hammam/gommage*)

Situated just a few doors down from textile shop Scenes du Lin (see SHOP), Les Secrets de Marrakech hasn't really been much of a secret in town since it opened to small but sustained applause a year or so ago. Small and compact it manages to pack a lot in, including a small boutique at the main reception (oils, sandals, straw bags, ladies clothing, knick knacks), a couple of treatment rooms that offer the usual run of facials, massages, lymphatic drainage and so on, and a *hammam*. You can even eat a light lunch on the terrace.

Spa Beldi, 6 Rue de Vieux, Gueliz
Tel: 0 24 44 91 78
Open: 9am–12.45pm, 3pm–7pm. Closed Sundays.
Price: 150dh (30 min massage), *hammam/gommage* 120dh

This spa was opened at the beginning of 2006 by Michelle Baconnier, the owner of the boutique a few doors down the road (see SHOP). Enter a nondescript façade and climb some stairs to enter the spa itself, which is compact – two treatment rooms and a small *hammam* – but clean and offers an odd décor combination of contemporary rustic (the treatment rooms) and old fashioned (black and white photos in gold frames). Treatments – noticeable for their use of pure, natural products – vary from massages (150 dh, 30 mins), waxing, manicures and pedicures, and face masks. Spa Beldi operates by appointment so make sure to call ahead.

La Sultana, 403 rue de la Kasbah
Tel: 0 24 38 80 08 www.lasultanamarrakech.com
Open: 10am–8pm daily
Prices: *hammam* 300dh (45 mins), massage 400dh (1 hour)

La Sultana not only has a quirky bar and a very fine restaurant (see page 96), it also has a great spa. Unlike the rest of the place, which can be slightly OTT, the spa is snug and sophisticated. Treatment rooms are arranged around a gorgeous jacuzzi (free with all treatments) and range from traditional *hammams* to facials and jet-lag treatments.

TOUR GUIDES AND PERSONALIZED SERVICES

Personal City Tour Guide

Mohammed Bouskri (tel: 0 61 14 74 82) has worked as a professional city guide for the past 35 years. He speaks fluent French and English and has shown many VIPs around the city, including Brad Pitt, Tom Cruise and President Nixon.

Personal Booking Service

Boutique Souk (tel: 0 61 32 44 75 / 0 61 32 44 73 www.boutiquesouk.com) is a bespoke Marrakech travel, concierge and events company specializing in concierge services for guests including restaurant, club, spa and personal shopping bookings.

Personal Shopping Guide

Dawn Boys-Stone (tel: 0 67 51 55 34 boysstones@goowy.com) has an intimate knowledge of all things related to the souks. Without taking commissions from the traders she'll guide you around the souks, shops and out-of-town outlets to help you find exactly what you want and at the right price.

Delphine Mottet (tel: 0 67 35 01 23) has lived in Marrakech for five years and knows Marrakech's shopping scene like the back of her hand. Fluent in French and English, she offers tailor-made half-day and full-day itineraries.

Personal Transportation Services

Marrakech Transport Travel (www.marrakech-transport-travel.com) is run by affable Moroccan gentleman Kamal, who can cater for your every transport need from weddings to week-long camping trips in the mountains.

TREKKING

The High Atlas begin just 50km from Marrakech, making it easy to hire a taxi and head out to the mountains just for a day or as long as you like. The best time to go is in the spring when the valleys are filled with wild flowers, or in the autumn when the summer temperatures have died down and the fruit harvests take place. Trek from village to village soaking up the traditional Berber hospitality and legendary bartering skills, or just the quiet and solitude that the mountains offer.

An ascent of Toubkal takes two days and affords the most amazing views at the summit. The best expeditions to the desert offer a unique insight into how the nomadic people subsist, and allow you to explore the barren landscape and experience its colours (as well as its loneliness).

Bivouac Erg Laabidlia, Centre M'hamid
Tel: 0 24 84 80 88/0 61 55 53 69 erglaabidlia@yahoo.fr

Run by the friendly Naji Labaalli, this place is located in what feels like the last place on earth – M'hamid. It's only worth contacting them if you've got a minimum of three days since they'll arrange for you to come from Marrakech to M'hamid, a day's journey, whence you have access to the desert. Naji owns desert bivouacs in Shakaga, which come equipped with cooks, showers, lavatories, and so on, and can organize walks, dune-climbs, camel rides and 4x4 tours. Camels are 300dh per day, jeeps 1,000dh per day, bivouacs 250dh per night (including lunch, tent and breakfast, hot showers and *hammam*, trips to the dunes, five days in the desert also a restaurant meal in M'hamid).

D and O Adventures
Tel: 0 24 42 1996 www.dandoadventures.com

Established by Canadian Dave McDougall and Frenchman Olivier Maillard, D and O Adventures specializes in adventure cycling. The company is based in both Quebec and Morocco, and with over 15 years of collective guiding and customized services between them, Dave and Olivier can arrange anything from day trips to two-week journeys through the mountains for all ages and skill levels. They also organize women-only excursions. See the website for departure dates and itineraries.

Destination Evasion, Villa el Borj, rue Khalid, Ben Oualid, Gueliz
Tel: 0 24 44 73 75/0 61 08 44 39 www.destination-evasion.com

Frenchman Pierre Yves Marais has been running excursions in Marrakech for five years, and knows his way around. He is able to tailor itineraries for groups or individuals ranging from a day trip to a week-long sojourn that takes in relaxed sightseeing, trekking through mountains and sleeping overnight in the desert. His veteran experience and ambitious packages and treks make his company one of the most reliable choices for any decent adventure in and around Marrakech.

Kasbah du Toubkal, Imlil, High Atlas
Tel: 0 24 48 56 11 www.kasbahdutoubkal.com

The Kasbah du Toubkal (see page 41), located next door to the village of Imlil, is a perfect starting-point for the ascent of Mount Toubkal. Staying here is a beautiful way to spend a few days and a great start and end to the arduous Toubkal climb or other walking and climbing options. All climbs and treks can be arranged through the Kasbah staff; prices range from 25dh per half-day trek to 200dh per person for a full ascent, all with guides, cooks, mules, accommodation and drinks (if required). The Kasbah recently built a stunning new trekking lodge, set even further in the mountains, overlooking a beautiful valley (see page 67).

La Pause, Douar Lmih Laroussiere, Commune Agafay, Marrakech
Tel: 0 61 30 64 94 www.lapause-marrakech.com

Built by eco-friendly Frenchman Frederic Alaime, La Pause (see SLEEP) is a surreal but beautiful place set in the Agafay Desert, 45 minutes from town. You can spend a few hours or a few days here, depending on your disposition, preferences and, of course, circumstances. Activities include crazy golf, horse-riding, trekking and cycling, and there's a small *hammam*, lunch and dinner options, as well as traditional Berber houses and tents for overnight stays.

Rak Express, 221 Avenue Mohammed V, Gueliz
Tel: 0 61 42 23 49 Rak-express@menara.ma

Moroccan owner Mohamed Helgane has worked for many tour companies and seems to have an infinite number of quality contacts on his books. He can take care of everything from hotel reservations to car hire, but also arranges day tours around the city (300dh per full day/200dh per half-day), mountain tours, desert journeys, camel-trekking, Berber trails (620dh including lunch) and day trips.

info...

CUSTOMS

Marrakech is a Muslim city, and no matter how laid-back it feels at times, it is still staunchly Islamic at heart. Certain rules should thus be followed, the main ones being to dress conservatively in religious places (and in people's homes), and if you would like to photograph someone, ask them first – women especially. Doing so should avoid causing offence. Many Muslims drink, most seem to smoke and drugs are also available, although penalties are severe for even the slightest drug offence.

DANGERS

Marrakech has an undeserved reputation for hassle. Stories abound of visitors being badgered from the moment they arrive in the country, but those days are long past. This is thanks to the Tourist Police, set up in 1999 to quickly remove and reproach anyone caught giving undue or unwarranted attention to a foreigner. You'll still be approached by persistent beggars and hard-sell hustlers, but they are generally easy to shrug off – a knowing smile works better than a stern face. If they do become overly persuasive just mouth the word 'police' and they should melt away. Failing that, cause a fuss and someone will usually appear to resolve the situation (Moroccans lose their temper easily but it hardly ever leads to violence and is just as quickly forgotten about). Also underserved is the city's reputation for being an unsafe place for foreign women. Many female ex-pats who have lived here for years speak only of respectful treatment by Moroccan men. Of course there are oglers and the occasional sly commentators, but these can easily be ignored. Pickpockets also sometimes operate in crowded areas – such as the Jemaa El Fna – so keep an eye on personal belongings.

MONEY

The dirham is the unit of currency for Morocco. It is possible to buy them in the UK (and elsewhere outside Morocco) although immigration may confiscate them since they prefer their currency to stay in the country. It's better to use ATMs while there (there are enough around to make it easy) or bring travellers cheques. At the time of writing, £1=16dh, €1=11dh, $1=9dh.

TRANSPORT

There is public transport outside the Medina (mainly buses and the occasional horse-drawn *caleche*) but it's much easier and more convenient to get around by taxi. Taxis come in two types: petit and grand. The petit is the main mode of transport for short distances (within the city). They are small, light-brown cars (often Fiats) that, just in case, have the word 'Petit' stencilled onto their roof-racks. They are ubiquitous and inexpensive, with a ride from the Medina to Gueliz, for example, costing around 10dh. However, half the drivers are the biggest chancers in town. Many honest ones will simply click on a meter, but many will claim it's broken or just ignore you if you ask. Two things can happen here: either they are honest and genuinely don't operate with a meter (and will simply charge you the correct fare); or they will try and overcharge you. It's a perennial frustration but often best to simply hail another cab if a driver refuses to meter the ride. Minimum fare is 5dh. Grand taxis are bigger, estate-style cars and mainly used for large groups or long journeys out of town.

TELEPHONES

All numbers given in this book exclude the international dialling code but include the Marrakech city code. To call any number from Marrakech simply dial as written. To call Marrakech from the UK, dial 00 212 followed by 24 for Marrakech. To telephone from a public phone look out for the coin-operated tele-boutique booths (marked by a large blue and white sign) or the orange card-operated phones. Cards can be bought from newsagents or post offices. Mobile coverage in Marrakech is on the whole very good – just remember to have your international dialling option activated.

TIPPING

Tips in restaurants should be around 5–10% depending on the level of service. For taxis, if they give you a fair price and use the meter give the drivers a decent tip or simply round up; for those that don't use the meter give them nothing extra.

L'ABYSSIN 72, 73
Agafay desert 47, 184
Agdal Gardens 136, 144–5
Ahmed Ait Taleb 159–60
Akbar Delights 155
Akkal 168
alcohol 13, 100–1, 125, 186
L'Amandier see Le Square
Amandine 114
Amanjena 30, 31
Amanjena Boutiques 155
Amanjena Spa 179
Amanjena Thai 71, 72, 74
Ambiance & Styles 164–5
Amira 160
Arab village 32–3
art 21, 85, 120, 137, 143–4, 149, 152–3
Art & Deco (Chez Alaoui) 168
Art Akhnif 158–9
Artisan El Koutoubia 161
Atelier Moro 155–6
Atika 160
Atlas Karting 177–8
Ayniwen 28–9, 30, 31–2
Azziza 169

BADII PALACE 136, 138
Bagatelle 75
Bahia Palace 138–9
Bains de Marrakech 17, 179
bars 20, 92, 100–11
    prices 101
Bazaar les Palmiers 159
Beldi 156
Beldi Country Club 25, 114–15
Bellawi 167
Ben Youssef Medersa 139
Berber villages 66–7, 173, 177

Bijouterie El Yasmine Abdelghani 171
Bivouac Erg Laabidlia 182
Bô-Zin 71, 72, 75–6, 102
Boule de Neige 115–16
Bouskri, Mohammed 58, 184
Boutique Indigo 156
Boutique Souk 184
Boys-Stone, Dawn 185

LA CABANE D'ALI BABA 167–8
Café Arabe 116
Café de France 113, 117–18
Café des Epices 117
Café du Livre 113, 118–19
Café les Negoçiants 113, 119–20
cafés 112–23
    breakfast 113, 115–16, 117, 121
    brunch 81, 119
    gelateria 114
    lunch 116, 121
    patisseries 112, 114, 115, 122, 123
    salons de thé 114
    vegetarian 122
calligraphy courses 54
car hire 183
Caravanserai 29, 32–3
Casa Mangani 161
casinos 125, 133–4
Cavalier Ranch 176
Centre Artisanal 153
Centre Commercial 154
Churchill's Piano Bar 102–3
city tours 183, 184
Le Club 92
Club Equestre de la Palmeraie 176–7

Le Comptoir 71, 76–7, 103–4
cookery schools 51, 174–5
Creation et Passementerie 157
Crystal 77–8
customs 186
cycling 47, 67, 183–4

D AND O ADVENTURES 183–4
dangers 186
Dar Attajmil 33–4, 179–80
Dar Cherifa 112–13, 120
Dar Doukkala 34–5
Dar El Bacha 36
Dar les Cigognes 35–6
Dar Liqama 174
Dar Marjana 13, 71, 78–9
Dar Moha 13, 71, 72, 79–80
Dar Saria 36
Dar Tiskiwin 142
Dar Zellij 80–1
Dar Zemora 28–9, 37
dars 28
desert 9, 47, 182–3, 184
Destination Evasion 182–3
Diamont Noir 126
drugs 186

EL BADIL 151
El Fassia 71, 72, 81–2
El Massraf 115
Ensemble Artisanal 154
Es Saadi casino 125, 133–4

FAN WA NOUR 161
film 137
fitness centres 31, 46, 58
Le Foundouk 71, 82

index

GALERIE BIRKEMEYER 170
Galerie d'Art Lawrence-Arnott 143
Galerie Mourjana 151
Gallerie Bleu 137, 152
gardens 136, 137, 144–7
golf 24, 25, 175–6
Golf d'Amelkis 25, 175
gommage 173
Grand Café de la Poste 113, 120–1
grand taxi 187
Gueliz 20–3, 101, 149

HADIKA 83
haggling 148–9
hammam 17, 172–3, 179–82, 184
Hammam Nikhil 180
Hassan Makchad 162
High Atlas Mountains 9, 33, 40–2, 67, 173, 182
history 8, 16, 20, 147
Hivernage 20–3, 101
hookahs 113
horse-riding 25, 176–7, 184
hotels 16, 28–68
  booking 29
  dars 28
  rates 29
  riads 8, 13, 28
  style, atmosphere, location 30
  top ten 30

IMLIL 41–2
Interieur 165

LE JACARANDA 84–5
Jad Mahal 71, 72, 86–7, 104–5, 126–7

Jamade 162
Jana 77
Les Jardins de la Koutoubia 30, 38, 83–4, 109
Les Jardins de la Medina 85–6, 180
Jebel (Mount) Toubkal 41–2, 173, 178, 182, 183
Jemaa el Fna 12, 13, 16, 72, 87, 140
Jnane Tamsna 28–9, 30, 38–9, 71, 72, 88

KAINKILA BOUGAGE 171
karting 177–8
Kasbah Agafay 29, 30, 39–40, 173, 174
Kasbah du Toubkal 29, 41–2, 67, 173, 183
Kasbah Tamadot 40–1
Kech Mara 71, 89
Kif Kif 162–3
Koutoubia Mosque 16, 136, 140–1
Kozybar 90, 100–1, 105–6
Ksar Char-Bagh 29, 30, 42–3, 71, 90–1
Kssour Agafay 101, 106
Kulchi 157

LES LAMPS D'ALADIN 165
libraries 120
Lolo Quoi 71
Le Lounge 107
Lun'Art Gallery 165

LA MAISON ARABE 43–4, 91–2, 174
Maison de Bali 166
La Maison du Kaftan

Morocain 170
Maison Mnabha 44–5
Majorelle Gardens 137, 143, 145–6
La Mamounia 45
  casino 125, 134
  gardens 137, 146
  maps
    Gueliz 22–3
    Hivernage 22–3
    Marrakech 10–11
    The Medina (North) 14–15
    The Medina (South) 18–19
    La Palmeraie 26–7
Marché Central 21
markets 21
  see also souks
Le Marrakchi 92–3
Marrakech 8–11
Marrakech Arts Gallery 152
Marrakech Film Festival 137
Marrakech Transport Travel 185
massage 50, 64, 179, 180, 181
Matisse Gallery 137, 153
The Medina 8–9, 28, 100–1, 136
  North 12–15
  South 16–19
Mega-Quad Excursions 178
Menara Gardens 147
Meryanne Loum-Martin Boutique 157–8
Michele Baconnier 158
Milouad El Jouli 158
Ministero del Gusto 166–7
money 150, 186
Montecristo 107–8, 127
Mottet, Delphine 185
Mount Toubkal 41–2, 173, 178, 182, 183

Moustapha Blaoui 167
Musée d'Art Islamique 143–4
Musée de Marrakech 144
museums 142, 143–4
music 81, 101, 125

NARWAMA 93–4
New Feeling 128–9
Nid' Cigogne 121–2
nightclubs 20, 124–33
  gay venues 126
  prices 125
  sex industry 124
Nikki Beach 25, 108–9, 122–3

OLD CITY SEE THE MEDINA
L'Orientalist 152
Original Design 163
Oukaimeden Ski Resort 178

PACHA 77–8, 124, 129–30
Palais Rhoul 28–9, 30, 46, 156, 180–1
La Palmeraie 24–7, 28
Palmeraie Golf Palace 25, 175, 176–7
Paradise 130
Patisserie de Princes 123
La Pause 47, 173, 184
personalized services 184–5
petit taxi 21, 187
photography exhibits 120
The Piano Bar 109–10
Le Plage Rouge 110–11
La Porte d'Orient 151–2
Pottery Souk 168

private planes 46
public transport 187

QUAD BIKING 178

RAK EXPRESS 185
restaurants 13, 17, 20–1, 42, 70–99, 77–8
  Asian 76
  delivery service 95
  food, service, atmosphere 72
  French 75, 76, 82, 84–5, 96–7
  fusion 95
  Indian 94–5
  Italian 76, 82, 98–9
  Moroccan 70–1, 76–7, 78–82, 83–4, 85–7, 89, 91–3, 96, 97–8
  prices 71
  seafood 78, 79, 83
  Spanish 83–4
  sushi 90
  Thai 71, 74, 85, 93–4
  top ten 72
  vegetarian 79
Riad 12 47–8
Riad 72 48–9
Riad Azzar 30, 49–50
Riad El Fenn 30, 50–1
Riad El Mezouar 51–2
Riad Enija 30, 52
Riad Farnatchi 30, 53
Riad Ifoulki 53–4
Riad Kaiss 54–5
Riad Kniza 55–6
Riad Lotus Ambre 56
Riad Lotus Perle 30, 57–8
Riad Lotus Privilege 58–9
Riad Mabrouka 59
Riad Mehdi 17, 60

Riad Tchaikana 60–1
Riad Tizwa 61–2
Riad W 62–3
riads 8, 13, 28
Riyad El Cadi 30, 63–4
La Roseraie 177
Royal Club Equestre de Marrakech 177
Royal Golf Club 25, 175–6
Royal Palace 16
Ryad Dyor 64–5

SAADIAN TOMBS 121, 141–2
Salam Bombay 94–5
Scenes du Lin 163
Les Secrets de Marrakech 181
shopping 21, 148–71
  antiques 21, 149, 151–2, 158, 159
  art 152–3
  artisans' markets 115, 149, 153–4
  books 118
  boutiques 149, 150, 154–8
  carpets and rugs 158–9
  footwear 148, 159–60
  furniture 21, 150
  haggling 148–9
  home decoration 150, 160–4
  home furnishings 164–7
  hours of business 150
  jewellery 167–8
  money 150
  personal guides 185
  pottery & ceramics 168–9
  Sidi Ghanem 150
  souks 13, 16, 148
  traditional clothing 148, 169–70

index

traditional handicrafts 171
Sidi Ghanem 150
skiing 178
smoking 46, 186
Souk Cuisine 17, 174–5
souks 13, 16, 148
Spa Beldi 181
spas 17, 150, 172, 179, 180–2
sport 172
Le Square 95
squash courts 45
La Sultana 65–6, 96, 181–2
Sur Une Ardoise 72, 96–7
swimming pools 122–3, 150, 173

TAGADERT 66
taxis 21, 150, 187
telephones 187
tennis courts 31, 39, 40, 45, 150
Theatro 131
Tigmi 29, 66–7
tipping 187
Le Tobsil 13, 71, 97–8
Totem 131–2
Toubkal Trekking Lodge 67–8
tour guides 183, 184
Tourist Police 186
transportation services 46, 183, 185
La Trattoria di Giancarlo 98–9
trekking 47, 67–8, 176, 182–4

VIA NOTTI 163–4
Villa des Orangers 30, 68
Villas of Morocco 69
VIP 132–3

YAHYA 164
yoga 40